CLASSROOM TIME MANAGEMENT

BOOK I: ORGANIZING SELF AND OTHERS

Revised Edition

Dick Webster
Dave Bailey

Webley Associates, Rochester, Minnesota 55902

The editors were Dr. E. Gershon, Warren Zimmerman, and Darla Olson.
The cover was designed by Doug Case and his high school students.
Modern Press was the printer and binder.
Published by:

Webley Associates
937-7th Avenue S.W.
Rochester, MN 55902
(507) 288-8074
If no answer, call (507) 282-7834

CLASSROOM TIME MANAGEMENT

Book I: Organizing Self & Others

ISBN 1-881449-00-9

ABOUT
THE AUTHORS

Dick Webster is presently a retired Staff Development Coordinator, K-12, from the Rochester Independent School District 535. Currently, he is on the adjunct staff for Winona State University, teaching graduate classes on "The Improvement of Instruction. "He taught physical education Pre-K through high school, directed health and physical education programs K-6 for 16 years, coordinated athletic programs K-12, and was the director of the Winona State University Graduate Induction Program for three years.

Dave Bailey is presently a Clinical Supervisor for the Winona State University Graduate Induction Program K-6. He has supervised over 30 student teachers and taught grades 6, 5, and 3. He was one of the eleven selected for the Minnesota Education Association's 1991 Teachers of Excellence. In addition, he has taught numerous staff development and college classes in the areas of Peer Coaching, Cooperative Learning, and Time Management.

BOOK I   Organizing Self and Others

CLASSROOM TIME MANAGEMENT

Book I Organizing Self and Others

Book II Organizing Students

Book III Organizing Work

NOTE TO TEACHERS

This book is made up of many ideas which are effective to different styles of teaching. The same skill or activity may be done in a number of different ways and still be time-efficient and effective for a teacher.

The real purpose of this book is to share some of the time-efficient and effective ideas of teachers so that other teachers can use them, modify them, or brainstorm other ideas from the ones given; in order to develop better classroom time management.

There are not enough hours in the day to do all the things that could be done in teaching, but maybe this book will help you be more time-efficient and effective with one or two of your current practices; so that in the end, this book will have been worthwhile to you.

THESE TIMESAVING IDEAS ARE BAR-CODED: **K-2** ON **TOP ONE THIRD**, **3-4** ON **MIDDLE THIRD**, and **5-6** on **BOTTOM THIRD OF EACH PAGE**. IDEAS WHICH ARE ESPECIALLY APPLICABLE TO **ALL GRADES K-6** ARE **NOT BAR-CODED**. PLEASE BE AWARE THAT MANY OF THE IDEAS SHARED BY TEACHERS TRANSCEND ACROSS SEVERAL GRADE LEVELS. BE SURE TO READ **ALL** THE GRADES' SUGGESTIONS IN ORDER TO PROFIT FROM THE MANY OTHER EXCELLENT IDEAS.

Teachers described these timesaving ideas to us in detail. The ideas have been condensed purposefully to save your time. The main ideas are presented to you in a manner that should expedite your time. You may adapt them to your style and teaching situation.

It is our sincere wish that you will find several entries to save you time in many areas and make your profession the most enjoyable.

DEDICATION

We would like to dedicate this book to all the excellent teachers of Independent School District 535, Rochester, Minnesota, in remembrance of all their years of past, present, and future professional dedication.

From all the information received, there were three main themes that emerged over and over again from the majority of teachers interviewed. First, all of these teachers put many **extra** hours into their workday beyond the "required" time. Second, **planning**, both short- and long-range, was a very important part of their teaching schedule. Third, the use of students to do many of the daily tasks was developed through **direct teaching** of the **skills of independence** to students at grade levels K-6.

ACKNOWLEDGEMENTS

There were over one hundred teachers who made this book possible. The first group of teachers, who provided their expertise and ideas, are listed on the next page.

The second group of teachers, who shared their expertise and ideas, wished not to have their names listed.

The last group of teachers are those who were not asked to share their ideas due to time restrictions, but would have shared their ideas if asked.

A special "Thank You" to Warren Zimmerman, retired Elementary Principal, who assisted with the writing of the introductions to each chapter.

CLARIFICATION: Teachers were selected, by their grade levels (K-6), at each building, thus providing a mixture of teaching experiences.

Any errors in interpretations of the information given by teachers is unintentional.

TEACHERS CREDITED

Holly Anderson	Darlene Forbrook	Gloria Obermeyer
Joyce Anderson	Kathleen Freeberg	Herbert Ollenburg
Peggy Anderson	Bob Gray	Marlys Ostby
Sue Bock (Greenberg)	Bonnie Gunderson	Carol Passi
Ramona Back	Charles Healy	Bill O'Reilly
Bonnie Bailey	Diane Kinneberg	Linda Rud
Kim Benda	Kelly Kosidowski	Esther Schmidt
Bruce Bigelow	Jim Kulzer	Carol Schroedel
Barbara Campbell	Dorette Leimer	Phillip Settell
Janet Carstensen	Leo Loosbrock	Gwen Stanich
Rosemary Chafos	Scott Mahle	Joe Stanich
Jane Coy	Marilyn McKeehen	Bill Temple
Lois Crouch	Mary Beth Miller	Dorie Thamert
Betty Danielson	Nancy Mix	Tom Theismann
Char Davis	Evelyn Nauman	Arlene Thone
Joan Davis	Don Nelson	Lynn Tollar
Doris DeSart	Marilyn Norland	Jay VanOort
Tony Floyd		

Chapter I - Organizing Self

TEACHER PLEASE NOTE: Please be aware that many of the ideas shared by teachers can and do transcend across several grade levels. Be sure to read all grades' suggestions in order to profit from the many other excellent ideas.

INTRODUCTION

Each year I ask, **"How can I get better organized?"** I have organized myself over time and I still ask the same question each year.

Initially, you will need to spend more time during the beginning of the year. Time spent organizing oneself in the beginning yields multiple dividends later. Good organization will help you be more confident, have less stress, not duplicate work, not miss details, and you won't feel as rushed. There will be fewer problems to address with students, parents, peers, and administrators if you are organized.

"Time is like money. Investing in it ahead of time pays great interest later on."

Dave Bailey
A Rochester Teacher

NOTES:

"One gets a feeling of being more satisfied when you feel you are doing things more effectively and efficiently."

Don Valentine (1989)
A Rochester Principal

TWO MAIN AREAS	Schedule your time into two main areas: **School Time** and **Home Time**. Then keep them as separate as possible. If you take work home, you will end up doing it several times in your mind as well as the physical work. Do it **one time** at school and enjoy your free time at home.
EARLY A.M.	Getting up earlier in the morning will give you a more relaxed attitude and make you better prepared for those last minute emergencies such as a surprise staff meeting, the new student assigned to your room, the gathering of the materials you forgot to get around to yesterday, etc.
BEFORE YOU LEAVE SCHOOL	Write all of the next day's chalkboard material on the board before you leave at night. You won't be off schedule if something comes up the next morning, and a substitute will really appreciate it.
"MY DAY"	Select a Tuesday, Wednesday, or Thursday and call it **"MY DAY."** Make sure everyone understands that nothing will stand in the way of your doing what you want to that afternoon and evening after school. Reduce your stress with sports, reading, a show, etc.
ANALYZING YOURSELF	Create a personal **"mind set,"** promising yourself to analyze each part of your job and your role in it. Analyzing each thing you do will save time in the long run and provide more time for classroom activities, more creative ideas, extra time to work with students, etc. Set time aside to be proactive rather than reactive.
AFTER SCHOOL ROUTINES	Establish an efficient, after-school routine to keep yourself **"on track."** Save time by knowing what needs to be done and then comes the hard part: **doing it**. Perhaps a short pop break, plan tomorrow, check papers, and gather materials. Reevaluate your routines and habits regularly to see if they can be made more efficient.
ESTABLISH SPECIFIC TIMES	Set the **same time** each week for specific jobs to be done. For example, your newsletter, correcting, planning, etc. A routine is a time saver. You do it automatically; it isn't forgotten, and you don't do it piece meal---starting over several times.

(Organizing Self)

REFLECTION TIME	Set aside 5-10 minutes at the end of the day for reflection. Think about all the things done well, list them and date the papers to validate the positive. Attitude is 95% of most things!
NO "HOME" WORK	Don't bring home schoolwork if at all possible. Stay at school and finish what is necessary for the next day. Save the evening for yourself and family. You'll be happier and fresher the next day. Thinking about having to do the work you bring home is as tiring as actually doing it.
UNINTERRUPTED CLASSROOM TIME	If you are the type that needs uninterrupted time to yourself for planning, look for time to work in the room outside of the normal school day. It is more productive to work in the classroom than to take things home with you. All the materials are there and you can better visualize your intentions. It is a good feeling to leave everything at school and separate it from your family and personal time. Try staying later after school, coming in on weekend days, or arriving an hour earlier. (Also ask yourself if you are efficiently using special area teacher times and noon hours during the regular school day.)
TEAM MEMBER'S DESK	Team members should put their desks together for saving steps, easier communication, and increased planning time. Eating lunch at your desks together saves lots of time, too.
LUNCH BREAK TIME	Shorten your lunch break, or skip it all together. This added work time can get you out of the building earlier at night without the strings of correcting papers, planning, etc. attached to your off-duty time. This will give you more quality time at home with your family or to do relaxing things for yourself.
"YELLOW" PAD	Use a yellow pad of paper for detailed plans of the day. This makes it very easy to find amongst the many other papers in the room. The papers are bound so you don't run the risk of losing separate sheets, either.
ONE INSTRUC-TIONAL LESSON PER DAY	Plan out **one** of next week's major instructional area's lessons every day. This way, by Friday you'll have the major lessons all completed for the next week without having to do them all at once.

DEALING WITH MAIL

Try to read through your mail immediately when you get it. Throw the junk mail, record the important dates on your calendar, and throw the notices away. Try never to touch the same papers twice.

PLASTIC BAGS

Put manipulatives in see-through plastic bags and hang them on a nylon cord with clothespins. They are easy to see and remain neat and out of the way.

MASTERS

Set up a three ring notebook which holds all your **"masters"** to be copied. Index it with dividers by subjects and months. It is worth the time it takes in the years to come, having it all right at your fingertips. If a paper has three holes in it, it is easily identified as the master.

FILING MASTERS

When using master copies, make sure to put them back before they get mixed up with the student copies and are used. A trick is to tilt the file in the filing cabinet until you replace the master. It makes it easier to find and you don't forget because it acts as a reminder.

SEATING CHART

Make a blank seating chart just once. Cover with plastic and simply wipe off the out-of-date names and write in the current seating arrangement. Leave the chart in a prominent place for the sub. Grease pencil won't smudge as quickly as overhead projector pens.

DAYS' SCHEDULES

For students who can read, laminate the regular days' schedules and put them on a flip chart on the chalkboard. Any changes can be written in next to the regular times. That way you won't have to write the "normal" schedule everyday, and it helps to keep you and your students on track.

LARGE SCHEDULE CHART

Put the day's schedule on a large chart for yourself and the students to follow. Reuse the charts noting just the changes. Don't write the whole schedule completely over every morning.

*"One must find **their** best time to do work."*

Joe Stanich (1989)
A Rochester Teacher

COMMERCIAL CALENDAR

A commercial calendar system is available. The Day-Timer Plan/Manage/Memory System may be purchased from

> **Day-Timers,Inc.**
> **One Day-Timer Plaza**
> **Allentown, PA 18195-1531**

It is a planner/diary system which sorts out your activities by categories, appointments, "to dos," reminders, expenses, accomplishments, etc. Send for their free brochure.

START OF THE DAY

For middle and upper grades, set up a daily routine for the first 15 minutes of the day whereby students come in and a study period begins immediately. Have two sentences on the board for them to copy and proofread for mistakes. You can take attendance and get to individual problems first thing. It sets a business-like tone for the day.

JOBS TO BE DONE

List jobs to be done on a specific sheet of paper or calendar. Cross them out as you go for a visual reward to yourself. Divide large tasks into smaller subdivisions for easier management. Set up a **"tickler file"** to remind oneself of upcoming deadlines.

STUDENT WORKSHEETS

Run off copies of work for students well ahead of time. Have a volunteer or secretary run copies of worksheets, maps, etc. You won't get caught off guard if you plan ahead.

COLLECT/ HAND BACK PAPERS

Collect papers by rows and hand them back in the same order. Handing out a mixed pile of papers adds a lot of time and steps to someone.

END OF THE DAY

At the end of each day, write out the next day's schedule on half of a sheet of paper and on the other half list jobs to be completed by yourself (things to check on, materials, calls, etc.).

TARGET FOR SUCCESS

Each day take time to target for success the next day by making a more detailed plan for the next day's schedule from your weekly one. Color code daily events on the weekly schedule for easier reference, for example: spelling in yellow, change of students for different subjects in orange, math in green, etc.

Chapter II - Organizing Desk and Area

TEACHER PLEASE NOTE: Please be aware that many of the ideas shared by teachers can and do transcend across several grade levels. Be sure to read all grades' suggestions in order to profit from the many other excellent ideas.

INTRODUCTION

Each year I ask, **"How can I get better organized?"** I have organized myself over time and I still ask the same question each year.

First impressions and **efficiency** are the bywords for this chapter.

People judge you by your neatness and organization. People visiting your room for the first time will carry that impression with them for a long time. Don't embarrass yourself--stay organized.

You will be more efficient with an organized desk/area. You'll save time finding things and will be more prepared for a substitute teacher.

If your desk or work area piles up, you know you're behind in organizing and filing. The following entries should help the novice and the expert. It is an area that constantly needs attention.

"Each year ask yourself: How can I get better organized?"

Kathy Davis (1989)
A Rochester Teacher

"Don't spend time; invest it."

Anonymous

TEAMING DESK	Team teachers: Put your teacher desks face-to-face for easier communication and ease of handing material back and forth.
PART OF THE CLASS	Placing your desk into the regular class seating arrangement gives the feeling of being part of the class, more approachable, and less authoritarian.
GLASS TOP	Put a sheet of glass on your desk. It is easy to clean, provides a good surface to write on, and is an excellent place to put your daily schedule and calendar under. You can see them at a glance yet they are out of the way and do not get dog-eared.
LARGE DESK CALENDAR	A full-sized desk calendar is very useful to provide long-range planning. It is easy to see because of its handy placement right where you do lots of your weekly lesson planning, anyway. Just jot down important dates, plans, and ideas as they come in so that they are not forgotten later.
LAMINATED TAGBOARD FOR MESSAGES	Laminate a large sheet of tagboard for the top of your desk. It doubles as a blotter and a place to write messages to yourself. Use a marking pen. Others can leave you notes when you're not in the room. Everything is easily wiped clean with a damp cloth.
FILE CABINET	Save steps by placing a four drawer filing cabinet right next to your desk. Magnetic holders work well to post things on it, too. Hint: File things sideways so that when you open the drawer you don't have to move backwards to see the alphabetical dividers. You are automatically looking at them straight on.
STUDENT MAILBOXES	Have your student **mailboxes** located next to your desk. It will save you steps while allowing you to keep a neater desk. They hand their papers into their mailboxes. You just reach over to retrieve, correct, and hand back their work. No problem with papers without names, either.
BOOKSHELF	Put your desk near a bookshelf or a shelf stack. This will save you many steps and time when looking for that curriculum guide, textbook, or other planning material while sitting at your desk.

(Organizing Desk and Area)

EXTRA TABLE TOP
Set a table or spare student desk next to yours. This gives you easy reach for those items your regular desk just isn't able to hold. Better organization is the goal here.

BOOKCASE ON TOP
Purchase or build a 3 foot book case or shelving on top of your desk. It allows increased storage at an arm's length away. Those extra steps take time.

SIDE OF FILE
Use the side of your metal files. Buy magnets to hold important memos, pictures, papers of all sorts. Better yet, put the files next to your desk--again, within easy reach.

PENCIL/ PEN CUP
Have a cup for pens and pencils. It works great as a lost and found and for those who forgot to sharpen their pencils at the proper time or can't find their pencil. Make it an exchange system: They put in their dull pencil in order to take a sharpened one. Have a student in charge of sharpening them all during a break each day. This cuts down on noise and wasted time.

CONTAINERS
Use cups or containers to separate pens, pencils, magic markers, small paper clips, etc. Have some for students and some for yourself. A lost and found is a good catch all.

CLIPBOARD
Use a clipboard for the daily attendance sheet(s). It is handy to carry with you, provides a good writing surface, and the slip(s) do not get lost in the paper shuffle if you clip them in as soon as you get them.

EASY ACCESS
Arrange your desk area so that everything is within easy reach. You shouldn't have to get up to get files, curriculum guides, papers, etc. Place a table adjacent to your desk, with files and cabinets close by; try to have a bookshelf behind or to the side of you, and keep everything you use often within 360 degrees and easy reach.

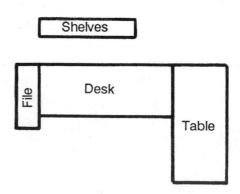

**STUDENTS'
AREA**

Designate **part** of your desk for students to staple, tape, etc. Don't let them take over all areas, or you won't have any room left.

**PAPERS TO
OTHER AREA**

To keep your desk top cleaner and easier to use, have students hand papers into other areas in the room. Set up and label tubs, baskets, or areas of collection. Target, K-Mart, or Shopko sell stacking storage trays. Buy strong sturdy ones so they will last over the years without replacing.

**CLEAN
DESK TOP**

Keep your desk top clean and free of student notes, parent slips, permission slips, money collections, etc. Have a specific basket or place for each of these. Students will pre-sort them by putting them in the proper place; your desk will remain "useable," and they won't get lost in the shuffle.

**NEW UNIT
AREA**

Dedicate one area of your desk just for that new, special unit you're working on. Keep a collection of items for this theme in one place and it will be easy to remember and to get at when you have to.

**STUDENT
NOTES**

Keep one drawer just for copies of past student notes and parent communications. Many times verification is needed and a double check is wise. Once they're gone, it takes time to reestablish communication about a subject. The drawer can be cleaned out periodically.

**DISTRICT
NOTICES**

Keep one drawer for everything sent to you by the district and building. It provides a ready resource to refer back to for verification and information. The drawer can be cleaned out at the end of each school year.

**EXTRA
STORAGE**

Purchase baskets to sit on rollers. Each basket represents one subject. These can be moved around the room and separated for taking home. Include manuals, texts, worksheets, materials, etc.

**P.E. SHOE
STORAGE**

If you get 6-7 pop cases, a whole classes' phy. ed. shoes can be conveniently stored neatly in a small space. Three pair fit into each section. Put the names on the sides for easy identification.

PLASTIC TUBS

Use plastic tubs for each subject area. They are easy to move, provide a substitute teacher a sense of security, and would include recording sheets, teacher's edition, curriculum guide, support materials, etc. These may be purchased from any discount store.

EXTRA FILE SPACE

Use boxes for increased file space. Be on the outlook for boxes about 12 inches wide to act as open file drawers.

WEEK'S WORKSHEET STORAGE

Have a 5-slot divider for student materials gathered up ahead of time. Worksheets and materials go in the corresponding slot for each day of the upcoming week.

SILVERWARE DIVIDERS

A common silverware divider or cups work well to organize pens, pencils, paper clips, etc. A student work/material center will keep the traffic pattern away from your desk, teach responsibility, and eliminate hundreds of requests.

ORGANIZE IN-BASKET MATERIALS

Scan your in-basket materials and divide them immediately into three categories:

1) **DO IMMEDIATELY**
2) **DO SOON**
3) **PUT ON THE BACK BURNER**

FOUR CORNERS

Use the 4 corner system:
- Corrected papers in one corner
- Incoming papers in another corner
- Papers to go over individually in another one
- Papers and notes to be taken to the office would occupy the last corner

SUBJECT AREA BOXES

Organize teacher subject area boxes for each curriculum area, committees, correcting, computer software, handbacks, newsletters, volunteers, reference books, etc.

KEEP DESK TOP CLEAN

Keep your desk top clean and neat. Remember, first impressions by others is important. A psychological impression of a clean desk projects a person who is in control, knows his business, is working at his/her job, and is providing a good model for his/her students.

"Keep no papers on your desk."

Sue Bock (Greenberg)   (1989)

A Rochester Teacher

STACKING TEACHER'S MANUALS

Stack your teacher's manuals in order as they will be taught each day. This organization is especially time saving when teaching a combination classroom with such a variety of lessons.

FOLDER/DAY

Have a folder for each day of the week. Review and organize it for the next day. You won't have to shuffle through non-pertinent papers <u>and</u> you won't have all those papers on your desk.

COLOR CODE

Lay out each day's activities by subject on colored paper labeled the same as in the plan book. This will organize you and will be all set for a substitute, if needed.

BEFORE YOU LEAVE

Every day just before you go home, place three items on top of each other in the center of your desk: Grade/record book, Plan book, and Substitute teacher's folder.

CLEAR OFF DESK

Plan and set aside specific time to make sure your desk is cleared off once a week. Don't let materials/papers build up until the job looks too big to even start on. Your attitude will be better and the task will be more manageable.

DATED TIME LINES

Keep a special sheet of paper or date book right on your desk top for listing jobs to be done and specific time lines. Cross them out as you finish them. It is like a self-reward to see them being done. Stress decreases as you see accomplishments and progress.

DIVIDE LARGER TASKS

Divide larger tasks into smaller, more manageable ones.

TICKLE FILE

Use a **"tickler file"** system by writing reminders down in your calendar a week <u>ahead</u> of time. These reminders will **"tickle"** your memory of what needs to be done in the near future. You won't have as many harsh surprises and short lead times on required work.

"A place for everything and everything in its place."

Anonymous

NOTES:

"One of the best lessons that anyone can learn in life is how to use the time wisely. Consider what can be done in ten minutes. It will pay huge dividends."

William A. Irwin

Chapter III - Time Scheduling

INTRODUCTION

Each year I ask, **"How can I get better organized?"** I have organized myself over time and I still ask the same question each year.

Time is the most important item over which you have control. How you manage it is critical since it is finite. Everyone has the same amount. How you plan and follow through makes the difference.

Teachers in control exhibit a pattern of wisely spending time up front to schedule their time efficiently. Delegating, teaming, flexibility, and keeping a calendar are a few of the ideas explained in this chapter.

*"Time on task is not the same as **quality** time on task."*

Carol Cummings (1985)

NOTES:

"There are never enough hours in the day to do all

the things that <u>could</u> be done in education."

Ruth Morgan
A Rochester Teacher

NEVER ENOUGH TIME

There never will be enough time to do all the things you want to do. Once resigned to this fact, organization is your best ally. One must find their best times to work and schedule it in; perhaps come to school early or stay later. It is universally held that it is best not to take work home on a regular basis. A personal life away from school is important. It refreshes and adds dimension to your teaching. Use prep time to the maximum for correcting and planning. Develop techniques to tactfully free oneself from time-consuming, non-productive discussions.

THREE LEARNING MODALITIES

Establish learning centers using the three learning modalities. Recycling information already taught by using sight, hearing, and touch will solidify those concepts. Flashcards, filmstrip previewers, headsets, manipulatives, etc. are examples. Don't forget to supply extension activities to challenge the top students.

SPONGE ACTIVITIES

Use **"sponge activities"** for those frequent 5-10 minute slack periods. An educational group game using a recently taught concept, or other creative gimmick, is better than free time for the students to get "off track." Remember, 5 minutes wasted each day equals 2 1/2 total school days per year!!

"Always do what you expect----follow up on your expectations."

Steve Milburn (1989)
A Rochester Teacher

5-10 MINUTES

Don't wait for those larger half hours of prep time to do your personal work. Special area teachers' scheduled times are wonderful, but so are those 5 and 10 minute periods of "down time" that show up every once in awhile. Use the shorter periods of time wisely. Add them up and you get many hours of extra work time during the day if you use them to run errands, plan, write notes, organize your desk, file, make a phone call, etc.

YOUR BEST WORKING TIME

When is **your** best "working time?" Are you a morning or evening person? Establish your best working time and use it to do a little planning every day so that by Friday, the next full week's schedule is completed. The weekends will take on greater meaning and you will feel much more organized.

*"You need to schedule **your** work time the same as for students."*

Sue Bock (Greenberg)   (1989)
A Rochester Teacher

STAY AHEAD

Do not fall behind. Working a little everyday on paperwork, for example, is better than storing it up for the weekend. The feeling of playing catch up is stressful. Make a commitment to address what needs to be done each day. Stay ahead of the game.

INTEGRATE

Save on writing up too many lesson plans by not teaching every subject every day. Teach certain subjects on certain days. Integration of the curriculum will save making so many disjointed presentations.

LONG RANGE PLANS

If you get a district day or a large block of time each quarter to do reports, think about long range planning. Plan the next quarter's instruction, order worksheets, order films, gather materials, schedule field trips, contact speakers, and sketch in your lesson plan book for these units.

DOUBLING UP SNACK BREAK

If pressed for time you might try doubling up your snack break with a subject area. While the students eat their mid-morning snack, do some light correcting, project work, etc. with the students.

GETTING TO KNOW STUDENTS

Time spent can be time saved. Behavior problems may be diminished by scheduling yourself into the room during student breaks and noon hours where weather dictates that they stay inside. Getting to know the students better through listening and being part of the classroom family is important.

SET TIME ANNOUNCE-MENTS
Ask the principal and office not to overuse the P.A. System. Perhaps have a set time for announcements, unless they're a real emergency. Interruptions are usually not time-savers for <u>you</u>. They are a convenience for the office. Encourage more daily bulletin or memo communications.

TEAM ANNOUNCE-MENTS
One team teacher can do the opening announcements for all students while the other has an extra 15 minutes prep time. Switch off each week. No need to put out the same information more than once!

PLAN AHEAD FOR VOLUNTEERS
Establish a folder for your volunteer/educational assistant. Plan a week ahead for the items you wish to have done. It eliminates quick decisions and the time it takes to orally communicate everything.

ONE-TO-ONE CONFERENCES
Deviate from your regular schedule the week before parent-student-teacher conferences. Plan more independent work and films in order to free yourself up for any one-on-one student-teacher conferences.

STUDENT PERMANENT FILES
Update student profile cards and records before the end of the year. Any large job done in pieces is easier than all at once, especially at the end of the year. Sign all the folders ahead of time and just fill in the dates later.

T.V. CORRECTION TIME
Try correcting papers while you watch T.V. Commercials provide a lot of extra constructive time over the period of a school year, and simple items can even be corrected during the program.

SUMMER TIME
Use some of your time during the summer to prepare for the next school year at your leisure. It will pay you back in less stress and an intrinsic feeling of doing a better job. (Bulletin boards, running off materials ahead of time, making student games, learning stations, name tags, filing, organizing plan book, etc.)

STUDENT INDEPENDENT TIME
Try to keep a schedule as much as possible. It is good for you, and the students like consistency and knowing what comes next. It gives them a feeling of security to be able to depend on a routine. With a little encouragement, the students will even have their texts and materials out for the next subject before you say anything.

LOW READING GROUP

If you have several reading groups, schedule your low reading group first and schedule everything around that. If you have to skip a group, don't let it be this one. They need your help the most.

OLDER STUDENTS

Have older students read to the younger ones. The teacher does not always have to be "on stage." Use the time gained to your advantage. Tape recordings, partner reading, and listening stations are time savers as well as educational devices to teach cooperation, values, responsibility, etc., depending on the age of the children.

INDEPENDENT TIME SCHEDULE

Schedule an independent activity first thing each day. This will give you time to take role, check in folders, and conference on left-overs from the previous day. Students may make a good choice for themselves or you might assign a proofreading exercise, etc. depending on the age of the children.

MATH FIRST

Schedule math as the first subject of the day. It is structured to set the tone and usually has an assigned task to be done independently.

BEST TIME OF DAY

Try this schedule: Start teaching right away in the morning while the newness and motivation are at their prime. Save the afternoon for all the regular procedures, active learning, art, and more relaxing topics.

STUDY PERIOD

Schedule a block of time for students to be self-responsible. It can be a study period. Discuss the expectations so that you teach them how to handle their own time wisely. It frees you up to do some individual counseling, too.

TWO VS THREE GROUPS

If you have three reading groups, meet with your low reading group every day and the other two every other day. You will only have to meet with two groups per day. The one not meeting does the independent practice assigned the previous day.

MISTAKES

Save mistakes of students not following directions and put them in their "make up folder" to do with you, a parent, or independently at a later time.

REORDER WORKBOOK SHEETS

Pre-pull all student worksheets out of their workbooks and reorganize them in the order to be taught. Staple into units. These are easier to handle and no more messy notebooks.

STATION WORK	Station work is great for individual pacing and giving you more time to interact with smaller groups. More time on task with time for teacher observation results.
TOUCH PAPERS ONCE	A rule of thumb: **"Try to touch a paper only once!"** Think of the wasted time spent shuffling papers. Have students collect, correct, and pass back---not you.
THREE-RING BINDERS	Use a three-ring binder for your grade book, lesson plans, calendar, substitute folder, and meeting notes. It is especially handy to transport to home or meeting, everything is in one place, and pages may be removed as they become outdated. Just run off blank copies of a design you like for each section.
COLOR CODE CALENDAR	Color-code items in your personal calendar that will need to be done again next year. Then, simply copy those into your new one. It saves rethinking through all of the items and there is less room for forgetting. This works in the reviewing of lesson plans, too.
COMBINED PLAN BOOK & CALENDAR	Combine your lesson plan book with your calendar. Having only one place to look saves cross-referencing time. You will find you don't forget as many things and it makes planning easier, knowing what events and requirements are already scheduled for you.
STICKY NOTES	Use **"Post-it"** sticky notepads to write down items that need to be done for the day. They can be easily reprioritized, thrown away, changed, and even reused.
DATING INFORMATION	Put dates from notices, letters, bulletins, and communique directly into your personal calendar---then THROW THE BULLETIN AWAY! Don't collect papers you'll have to go through again. Keeping up with the daily input is better than trying to play "catch up" later on.
POCKET CALENDAR	Use a handy pocket calendar to keep your own schedule. Setting a definite time for certain tasks provides incentive to get started---the hardest part. It is such a good feeling to check them off as **DONE!**
A.M. WORK AT HOME	Do school work **at home** early in the morning before coming to school. It is hard to stay on task once you get to school due to social talking or other interruptions.

EARLY START AT SCHOOL
The early bird gets the worm. Getting to school early means you won't run into so many people to talk to. More concentrated work time, no line at the copy machine, availability of materials, and free use of the work room will allow you to get more work done in a shorter amount of time.

THINKING TIME
Set aside time just for personal thinking and planning time. If you don't build this into your schedule, you are not in charge and gains will be slower in coming. Take the initiative.

RIGID SCHEDULE
Set a rigid schedule for yourself and don't deviate from it. For example, work from 7:00 A.M. to 4:30 P.M. and don't look back. Just use your time wisely while you're at school. Many people work and eat at the same time, thus buying personal time for later in the day.

QUIET TIME
Schedule in some quiet, quality prep time by coming into school on the weekend. Home duties will distance themselves and most of the materials needed will be at your disposal.

LAMINATED SCHEDULE
Write a permanent schedule for each day of the week. Laminate it with holes to hang on two hooks in front of the room in a corner of the chalkboard. Changes can be written to the side as you flip it over each morning. You'll never have to write out the whole schedule for the day again. It is a prominent reminder for you as to what should be happening, too.

ANALYZE YOUR WORK
Analyze your traffic pattern. Do you make needless trips long distance to get materials that could have been gotten in one, if you were planning ahead? A good mind-set is to keep thinking a week in advance.

STUDENT HELPERS
Use students as your helpers for almost any job you need to do. Plan, teach, and evaluate their performance. Life skills are best taught when there is a real purpose and results can be seen.

TYPES OF CORRECTION
When correcting papers after school, do the ones with subjective, definite right or wrong answers first. You will be more alert and thoughtful if you save the objective, essay-type corrections until that evening or the next morning, after you have had some time to freshen up.

Chapter IV - Plan Book

INTRODUCTION

Each year I ask, **"How can I get better organized?"** I have organized myself over time and I still ask the same question each year.

Every effective teacher does good planning. Short range, long range, general, and specific; it acts as a necessary guide. Priorities are deliberately established and inclusions are based on sound education reasoning. There are always more choices than time will allow. Plan now for the most important ones.

Many time saving ideas about how to arrange and use your plan book are included.

"If you don't know where you're going, anyplace will do."

Anonymous

NOTES:

"To save time you must be well-prepared in not only what you teach (lesson plans), but also with supplies, materials, transition activities, etc."

Florence Swenson (1989)
A Rochester Teacher

MAKE A FORM/DAY	Set up a form for each day of the school week's cycle. This will prevent you having to fit the different schedules into a generic lesson plan book. Run copies and glue them in or make your own plan book with a three-ring binder. **(See Examples "A" and "B", pp. 32, 33)**
THREE-RING BINDERS	Make your own plan book using a three-ring binder. Run off masters of pages already labeled with times and area constants. Keep just a few week's plans or a complete quarter's in the book at one time, removing them as you finish. Add additional sections for grades, the year's calendar/appointment book, substitute folder, meeting notes, etc. It is easily organized and having everything in one spot makes it easy to find and carry. **(See Examples "C", "C1", "D", and "D1", pp. 34-37)**
TRANSPARENT POCKET	Place your weekly A,B,C,D,E day schedule inside a transparent plastic pocket. Just change the letters on the plastic each week to update the coordination with Monday - Friday. Use a marking pen which can be washed off easily. Using a three-ring binder allows you to pull out the units from the curriculum guides and put them in the plan book according to the next one. This way you have one book with everything in one place. **(See examples "E" and "E1", pp. 38, 39)**
OWN PLAN BOOK	Make your own plan book to fit what you want to teach, the order, information needed, etc. It saves all kinds of time by not having to write in all the same information. **(See examples "F" and "F1", pp. 40, 41)**
YOUR NEED	Develop your own book system to meet your needs at the Kindergarten Level. Don't limit yourself to someone else's generic layout. **(See examples "G" and "G1", pp. 42, 43)**
MASTER SCHEDULE	After you have established your normal weekly schedule for the year, make up a master page with specific times and subject areas for the full week. Reproduce this for each week of the school year. You will save many hours of work not rewriting the same times, labels, and information each time. You only fill in the new information such as concept, pages, materials, etc.

DETAIL LESSON PLANS

Put detailed lessons in a three-ringed binder according to subject and chronological order. Solid lessons can be reused or modified for the next time around without redoing them from scratch.

COLOR CODE DAYS

Use a blank sheet each day (M,T,W,...or A,B,C...) and fill in the blanks. Use a different color for each day of the week. **(See examples "H", "H1", "H2", "H3", and "H4", pp. 44-48)**

TEACHER'S TEXTBOOK

Keep a sheet of loose-leaf paper in each teacher's textbook. List what is to be taught in detail each day, related to the broad plan in the plan book. Update these sheets at the end of each day to keep current. These sheets give you much more room to write down those things you want to make sure not to forget.

PRE-LAY OUT FORM

Use a pre-lay out form developed for your specific reading groups. It saves extra writing time and takes the place of that part of the plan book. **(See example "I", p. 49)**

LARGER PAGE

Put your lesson plans on an extra large sheet of paper (18" x 11"). Have different schedules run off for different days. This extra space allows for special students' schedules, reminder notes to yourself, material needs, announcements, etc.

BLANK PLAN

Run off copies of blank plans (with appropriate headings, times, and special areas in place) on larger sheets of paper. In this way you will have more room to write and it will be easier to read. Enlarging machines or copy machines using 11" x 17" paper are ideal. Include:

> 1) **Objective or concept,**
> 2) **Materials and page numbers to be used, and**
> 3) **Expectations of guided and independent practice for each lesson.**

LONG WAY VS BOOK STYLE

Reconstruct your plan book to be used the long way versus the book style, right and left pages. Run off two pages (A.M. & P.M.) for the year. Glue them in as you go. **(See example "J" and "J1", pp. 50, 51)**

GENERAL PLAN	If you have trouble fitting everything into those small boxes in your lesson plan books, just sketch out the general plan there and write a brief, up-to-date, more detailed plan each day. Keep it on a clipboard for easy reference, checking off things as they are accomplished. It also gives you more room for notes, "to dos," etc. **(See example "K", p. 52)**
MATERIALS LIST	Have a separate sheet of paper right in your lesson plan book for keeping track of materials you'll need to get for the week, orders that you will need to make, and errands that need running. Fill it in at the same time you do your lesson plans so you won't have to rethink it through again later.
MONTHLY REMINDERS	Use the extra pages at the end of your Plan Book to divide into fourths. Label them by school months. Jot down important reminders for the future.
ORGANIZE DOWN VS ACROSS	For a change of pace and saving of flipping pages, you might try ruling your lesson plan books vertically instead of horizontally. Reading downwards throughout the day versus across will keep you on the same page.
ONE PAGE PER DAY	Use one whole page or sheet of paper for each day. Times and headings are done once and copies run off for each day. The extra room to write is great.
SPECIAL PAGES	Reserve the first few pages for important, non-changeable items such as class list, seating arrangement, birthdays, schedule, school calendar, etc. They are easy to find and help a sub out. Don't forget a schedule of which students see which special area teacher at what time(s).
ABBREVIATED DAILY SCHEDULE	Make an **abbreviated daily schedule** on a small strip of paper. It gives a brief outline to be copied and used for your plan book, substitute folder, an office copy, for students to tape to their desks, for parents at open house, special area teachers, etc. **(See example "L", p. 53)**
DATES FOR THE YEAR	Sit down one time and put in all the dates and known variables for the entire year. Those little minutes during the year add up to frustration. Do it all at once and forget it. Include student birthdays into your plan book at the first of the year, adding new students as they enroll. You won't forget to schedule those important events again. It acts as a "tickler file."

BE FLEXIBLE	Since most lesson plan books are inaccurate after 10:00 A.M. Monday morning, avoid writing lengthy weekly plans. If you need a substitute, you'll have to call in or write more detailed plans for that day anyway.
3-DAY PLAN VS 5	Do you make so many changes by Thursday that you end up practically rewriting your lesson plans over for the end of the week? An easy solution is to just plan for three days at a time. You'll still have a good idea where you're going but you only have to write specific lesson plans for the three day cycle. Substitutes will appreciate the "fresh" plans, too.
ONE DAY SPECIFICS	Plan the basic goals for the week, but only write in the specifics for each following day. By doing each day's planning the night before, changes, crossing out, and rewriting can be minimized.
DATES	Fill in all dates of school, A,B,C,D,E day schedules, conference days, etc. Doing it all at one time saves you the weekly chore of doing it throughout the year.
PLAN ONE MONTH AHEAD	Plan one month ahead at a time. It is a manageable amount, and allows you to see where you are going and to start thinking about resources you might want to use. Map out blocks of time and those times that will be taken up with special area teachers, conferences, birthdays of students, duty schedules, meetings, field trips, etc.
FILL IN THE BLANK	Write everything out in your plan book that you will regularly need, and then all you have to do is circle the area or fill in the type of activity or page numbers. **(See examples "M" and "M1", pp. 54, 55)**
SPECIAL INFORMATION	Insert special information into the front and back of your plan book. The school calendar can be in the front. Set up a teacher's notes sections in the back to jot in important information and reminders so that when planning your next week/month you won't forget to include these ideas or jobs in your plans. Include the seating chart, class list, birthdays, telephone numbers of parents and frequently called places, special area schedules, staff names, hot lunch prices, etc. Fill in all the "special" days of the year. Use a colored pen to make them stand out. Leave the last column on the side for short range TO DOs, ideas, brainstorms, etc.

WORKSHEETS

Put worksheets to run off and plans to do for next week in the back of your lesson plan book. Once a week, reorganize those papers and jot down the next week's plans in order as applicable.

LABELS AHEAD SUBJECTS/ TIMES

Type up labels for all subjects and times. Run off many copies. Glue or staple these into the plan book so that you only have to write in the assignments. This saves all the time of writing in subjects and times for each day, all year long.

SEPARATE PRE-HEADING

Use a separate pre-headed form for each reading group. This gives you more space to plan in detail for several groups. It is easier for a substitute to follow, can be kept right in your teacher's edition, and is less bulky.

SUB-DIVIDE

Sub divide the plan book into smaller squares for each subject. Dates, page numbers, week number, and number of days left of school can be added ahead of time (possibly during summer vacation).

ANNOUNCE- MENTS AND NOTES

Have a place for writing announcements or taking notes for the next day or week, right at the bottom of your plan pages. Simply cross them off as you go through the week. It is always at the forefront of your mind.

COLOR DOT FOR MATERIALS

Put a red dot in front of materials that will have to be run off. It acts as a visual reminder. You won't be caught off guard if you get your copying requests in ahead of time.

COLOR CODE SUBJECTS/ GROUPS

Color code each subject and group. Then have a bucket with the same corresponding color code to hold materials needed for that subject or group. It organizes yourself and is great for a sub.

A.M. AND P.M. PLAN

Put your A.M. plans on a different colored paper than your P.M. plans. They will be easier to find and you have only half as many papers to handle at a time.

USE HIGH- LIGHTER

Code your plan book with symbols and colors. A check means completed; circle if you didn't do it; and an arrow might mean to carry it over to the next day. Colors can secretly tell you which reading or math group needs extension or remedial work. Make up your own keys and symbols for quick locating and easier planning.

USE PENCIL FOR CHANGES Use pencil so that you can change and revise as needed. Things stay neater, easier to read, and color-codings stand out more.

HELP FOR SUBS Include special area and volunteer names in the plans. Substitutes need this and it is a nice reminder for yourself.

STICKIES Write specifics down on Post-it stickies which can be pulled off and stuck in place again for the next week's plan page. This saves the time of re-writing specifics each week.

CODING ( ) ( ) Check off items completed (✓) and use an arrow pointed to the next day for items not completed (-->).

LEARNER OUTCOMES AND SUBJECT FOLDERS Prevent a messy plan book filled with arrows and rewritings. Just put the Learner Outcome number and objective in your plan book. The rest of the information is in folders by subject area. The specifics are found here and are sequential so that they don't have to be changed.

SPECIAL AREA PLANS By keeping all special area lesson plans in your plan book, you can be more aware of and reinforce those concepts in your lessons. Integration of several subject areas adds to long-term memorization and transfer of learning.

LONG-TERM MEMORY Plan in for long-term memory of important skills. After a skill is taught, practiced, and tested; look ahead and select a time that would be good to review that specific skill. Build that activity in before you forget about it.

SAVE OLD LESSON PLANS Save your old lesson plan books. For areas that are consistent; cut, glue or staple into new book. For example, Phy. Ed. lessons to be followed up on from special area teacher.

LAST YEAR'S PLAN BOOK Look over your last year's lesson plan book every few weeks. It helps you monitor your progress compared to last year and jogs your memory as to what worked well and you might want to be sure to include again this year.

A.V. FOR NEXT YEAR Record or paste in Audio Visual Aides, along with the order numbers. Keeping your lesson plan book allows you to readily find this information the next year. Put comments beside the entry as a reminder of what was "+" or "-" about them.

DEVELOP REUSED LESSON PLANS

Reuse lesson plans several years in a row. Plan reading groups by levels as to what can be covered or completed in one day. Keep them in a folder by units and levels. They can be used sequentially with slight changes to meet individual class differences. The extra time spent developing them the first year will more than be made up for the next year.

HOME THINKING TIME

Duplicate your lesson plans to keep at home. Some of your best thinking is done without the pressure of the day. It's handy if you are ill, as the sub's copy will always be at school, yet you have a working copy when you need it.

COMPUTER PLANS

Put everything on your computer. Set up a schedule for each of the days of the week or A,B,C,D,E,F Day Schedule. Simply make the few changes in activities and let the printer do the rest. **(See examples "N" and "N1", pp. 56, 57)**

COMPLETE PLAN BOOK

There is a very complete booklet which can be purchased for $9.95. It includes a basic introduction to the booklet, sub information, a monthly calendar for events to be written in, an overview page for assignments of a 5-week period, goals and materials page for the week, meeting and conference page for the week, regular weekly lesson plan blanks, and an evaluation space for the end of each day. It may be purchased from:

Plan-It   by Richard Gloub
American Teaching Aids   ISBN #0-933965-00-1
Covina CA 91722

PURCHASE A PLAN BOOK

Two recommended commercial plan books available may be purchased from either:

Lesson Plan Book
Creative Teacher Press, Inc.
Hunting Beach, CA 92649

OR

Rulan Publishers   by Harlan Hanson
P.O. Box 24377
Minneapolis, MN 55424

"A goal is a dream with a deadline."

Steve Smith
Amdahl Corporation

```
AAAAAAA
AA    AA
AAAAAAA                Notes:                    Date:_____
AA    AA
AA    AA
```

DOL 8:45-9:00	ART 9:00-9:50	Reading 9:50-10:30			Recess 10:30-10:50	Math 10:50-11:20
		Red	Blue	Green		

Positive Action 12:15-12:30	Music 12:30-12:55 Phy.Ed. 1:00-1:30	Language Arts 1:30-2:15	Prim. Int. Curriculum 2:15-3:00

Date:_____

Writing to Read

Computer	Journal	Typewriter	Primary Editor

Listening	Teacher	Seatwork	
===========	=========	==========	==

Notes:

Page_____ A.M. Week of _____ Week_____

	MONDAY			
MONDAY				
TUESDAY				
WEDNESDAY				
THURSDAY				
FRIDAY				
NOTES				

Page_____ P.M.   Week of _____

	MONDAY				
MONDAY					
TUESDAY					
WEDNESDAY					
THURSDAY					
FRIDAY					
NOTES					

Week of _____

	8:45-:55	8:55-9:00	Reading Group 9:00-9:25	Reading Group 9:30-9:55	Reading Group 10:00-10:25		10:35-11:00	11:00-11:15	11:15
AM MONDAY ( ) 8:40 Bell Rings	# of days we've been in school (Pets put slips in attendance box)	General Seatwork ★ See Monday's Label	① Review vocabulary words - see basket	① Review Vocabulary Words - See basket (SP) #	① Review Vocab. words - See basket (SP) #	Clean-Up time from Reading Groups, Seatwork, + Learning Centers		(Handwriting) Use Benji Tg# ___ Pg# ___	Pos. Act. Tg.
			(Closure) Sing song	(Closure) Sing song	(Closure) Sing song			(Closure) Benji's Trick	
AM TUESDAY ( ) 8:40 Bell rings	hot or cold (Pets for the Day • Feed Fish	General Seatwork ★ See Tuesday's Label	① Review Vocabulary words - See basket	① Review Vocab. Words - See basket (SP) #	① Review vocab words - See basket (SP) #	(Pets are the leaders)		(Handwriting) Use Benji Tg# ___ Pg# ___	Pos. Act. Tg.
			(Closure) Sing song	(Closure) Sing song	(Closure) Sing song			Benji's Trick	
AM WEDNESDAY ( ) 8:40 Bell Rings	+ Good Morning	General Seatwork ★ See Wednesday's Label	① Review Vocab. words - See basket	① Review vocab Words - See basket (SP) #	① Review Vocab. words - See basket (SP) #			(Handwriting) Use Benji Tg# ___ Pg# ___	Pos. Act. Tg.
			(Closure) Sing song	(Closure) Sing song	(Closure) Sing song			(Closure) Benji's Trick	
AM THURSDAY ( ) 8:40 Bell Ring	• Flag Pledge • Attendance + Lunch count • Calendar	General Seatwork ★ See Thursday's Label	① Review vocabulary words - see basket	① Review Vocab. words - See basket (SP) #	① Review vocab words - See basket (SP) #		10:25-10:30	(Handwriting) Use Benji Tg# ___ Pg# ___	Pos. Act. Tg.
			(Closure) Sing song	(Closure) Sing song	(Closure) Sing song			(Closure) Benji's Trick	
AM FRIDAY ( ) 8:40 Bell Rings	Opening Exercises	General Seatwork ★ See Friday's Label	① Review vocab. words - see basket	① Review Vocab words - See basket (SP) #	① Review Vocab words - See basket (SP) #		10:30-10:35 Lavatory Break	(Handwriting) Use Benji Tg# ___ Pg# ___	Pos. Act. Tg.
			(Closure) Sing song	(Closure) Sing song	(Closure) Sing song			(Closure) Benji's Trick	

NOTES

36

IDEAS TO INCLUDE IN YOUR THREE-RINGED BINDER

**Section off with tabs or dividers:

I   **Lesson Plans**
Use your own original design; make a master with consistent headings, times, routines, etc. and then just run copies to eliminate repeating the same things each week.

II   **Grades**
Put student names on a grid class list. Alphabetize by <u>first</u> names for faster locating. Run many copies, color coding the paper for each quarter.

III **Year-long Calendar/Appointment Section**
Record things **once** and throw away bulletins, directives, appointment slips, etc. Use it as a "tickler file" to remind you of upcoming commitments.

IV   **Substitute Teacher Folder**
Include routines, discipline plan, building layout, procedures, staff & class pictures with names, special area times, lunch menu, etc.

V   **Meeting Notes**
Never be caught without extra blank lined paper.

VI   **Your Choice**
Telephone numbers, schedules, office procedures, special area lesson plans, telephone directions, favorite sayings, you name it---you got it!

Dave Bailey, 1992
WEBLEY ASSOCIATES
938-7th Ave. S.W.
Rochester, MN 55902

Kindergarten

Week No._____

		Language Arts	Physical Development	Literature	Environment
Monday	Opening - Attendance, Calendar, Weather, Announcements, Daily Plan				Math Social Studies PIC Science Health
Tuesday					Math Social Studies PIC Science Health
Wednes day					Math Social Studies PIC Science Health
Thursday					Math Social Studies PIC Science Health
Friday					Math PIC

38

1989-90

Fine Arts	Perceptual	Social Emotional	Teacher Notes
Art -		Sharing	
Music -		Free Time	
Art -		Sharing	
Music -		Free Time	
Art -		Sharing	
Music -		Free Time	
Art -		Sharing	
Music -		Free Time	
Art -		Sharing	
Music		Free Time	

	Level —	Level --	Notes
B DAY	Introduce Read pp. ____ Skills TE pp. ____ Vocab ____ Comp ____ Decoding ____ Skill Pack pp. ____	Introduce Read pp. ____ Skills pp. ____ Vocab ____ Comp ____ Decoding ____ Skill Pack pp. ____	Introduce Read pp. ____ Skills T.E. pp. ____ Vocab ____ Comp ____ Decoding ____ Skill Pack pp. ____	
C DAY	Introduce Read pp. ____ Skills T.E. pp. ____ Vocab ____ Comp ____ Decoding ____ Skill Pack pp. ____	Introduce Read pp. ____ Skills T.E. pp. ____ Vocab ____ Comp ____ Decoding ____ Skill Pack pp. ____	Introduce Read pp. ____ Skills T.E. pp. ____ Vocab ____ Comp ____ Decoding ____ Skill Pack pp. ____	
D DAY	Introduce Vocabulary Read pp. ____ Skills TE pp. ____ Vocab ____ Comp ____ Decoding	Introduce Vocabulary Read pp. ____ Skills T.E. pp. ____ Vocab ____ Comp ____ Decoding	Introduce Vocabulary Read pp. ____ Skills T.E. pp. ____ Vocab ____ Comp ____ Decoding	
E DAY	Introduce Read pp. ____ Skills TE pp. ____ Vocab ____ Comp ____ Decoding ____ Skill Pack pp. ____	Introduce Read pp. ____ Skills T.E. pp. ____ Vocab ____ Comp ____ Decoding ____ Skill Pack pp. ____	Introduce Read pp. ____ Skills T.T. pp. ____ Vocab ____ Comp ____ Decoding ____ Skills Pack pp. ____	
A DAY	LIBRARY	READING		

Pos.

	Spec.	Theme	Math	Lang	Hand	Action	Spell
A DAY	Library 2:00	Sub. Theme ___ S.S. pp. ___ Science ___ T.E. pp. ___	Chpt.# ___ pp. ___ Enrich p. ___ Practice p. ___	Short Shots # ___ Worksheet # ___	Lesson p. ___	Unit ___ Lesson # ___ pp. ___	Unit ___ Pre Stretch Test
B DAY		Sub. Theme ___ S.S. pp. ___ Science ___ T.E. pp. ___	Chpt.# ___ pp. ___ Enrich p. ___ Practice p. ___	Short Shots # ___ Worksheet # ___	Lesson p. ___	Unit ___ Lesson # ___ pp. ___	Unit ___ Pre Stretch Test
C DAY		Sub. Theme ___ S.S. pp. ___ Science ___ T.E. pp. ___	Chpt.# ___ pp. ___ Enirch p. ___ Practice p. ___	Short Shots # ___ Worksheet # ___	Lesson p. ___	Unit ___ Lesson # ___ pp. ___	
D DAY		Sub. Theme ___ S.S. pp. ___ Science ___ T.E. pp. ___	Chpt.# ___ pp. ___ Enrich p. ___ Practice p. ___	Short Shots # ___ Worksheet # ___	Lesson p. ___	Unit ___ Lesson # ___ pp. ___	
E DAY	Art 10:40	Sub. Theme ___ S.S. pp. ___ Science ___ T.E. pp. ___	Chpt.# ___ pp. ___ Enrich p. ___ Practice p. ___	Short Shots # ___ Worksheet # ___	Lesson p. ___	Unit ___ Lesson # ___ pp. ___	Unit ___ Final Basic and Stretch Test

Week _____

Kindergarten Weekly Plan

Whole Language

M	T	TH	F

Perceptual Motor:

**DAP: Conferences
Rug Party on:**

Sm. Group: Calendar/weather

Teacher Act:

Aide/Mom:

Stations:

Music:

Additional Information:
(Wed Schedule on back:)

Self-directed Learning Room:

Week_____

Wednesday Schedule

Reading Block: 8:40-9:15 / 12:35-1:00

DAP/Perceptual Side	Self-directed Learning / Sm. Group Side
	Art/Cooking:

Whole Group Music:	ESP Person	A.M.	P.M.
1.			
2.			
3.	Other info:		
4.			
5.			
6.			

Lesson Plans

Day A _____   Date _____

Special Times and * Special Area Teachers

no ____ * Music - 10:30 - 10:55 (B + D days)

yes ____ * P. E. - 2:30 - 3:00 (A + E days) - gym

no ____ P. E. - 2:30 - 3:00 (B + D days) - gym

no ____ P. E. - 2:30 - 3:00 (C C day) - West playroom

maybe ____ * Art - 10:50 - 11:40 (A2 - day) - art room

no ____ * Library - Usually "B" day at 11:00 ___ or 1:30 ___

no ____ * Mrs. Bogan - counselor - 11:25

8:45 | Attendance, Pledge, Song, Announcements,
      Handwriting -

9:00 | Rotate Reading Groups -

10:00 | Break   10:10

10:30

11:00

11:40   12:00 Lunch

12:45 - Rotate Math Groups

1:30

2:30 | P.E.   3:00 - Work Period

44

Lesson Plans

Day **B**   Date _____

Special Times and *Special Area Teachers

<u>yes</u> * Music - 10:30 - 10:55 (B + D days)

<u>no</u> * P. E. - 2:30 - 3:00 (A + E days) - gym

<u>yes</u>   P. E. - 2:30 - 3:00 (B + D days) - gym

<u>no</u>   P. E. - 2:30 - 3:00 (C C day) - West playroom

<u>no</u> * Art - 10:50 - 11:40 (A2 - day) - art room

<u>yes</u> * Library - Usually "B" day at 11:00 ____ or 1:30 ____

<u>no</u> * Mrs. Bogan - counselor - 11:25

8:45 Attendance, Pledge, Song, Announcements,
      Handwriting -

9:00 Rotate Reading Groups -

10:00 Break   10:10

10:30

11:00

11:40   12:00 Lunch

12:45 - Rotate Math Groups

1:30

2:30 P. E.   3:00 - Work Period

Lesson Plans

Day __C__   Date _____

Special Times and *Special Area Teachers

__no__ * Music - 10:30 - 10:55 (B + D days)

__no__ * P.E. - 2:30 - 3:00 (A + E days) - gym

__no__ P.E. - 2:30 - 3:00 (B + D days) - gym

__yes__ P.E. - 2:30 - 3:00 (C C day) - West playroom

__no__ * Art - 10:50 - 11:40 (A2 - day) - art room

__no__ * Library - Usually "B" day at 11:00 ___ or 1:30.

~~maybe~~ * Mrs. Bogan - counselor - 11:25

8:45 | Attendance, Pledge, Song, Announcements,
       Handwriting -

9:00 Rotate Reading Groups -

10:00 Break   10:10

10:30

11:00

11:40   12:00 Lunch

12:45 - Rotate Math Groups

1:30

2:30 | P.E.   3:00 - Work Period

46

Lesson Plans

Day ___D___   Date _____

Special Times and *Special Area Teachers

__yes__ | * Music - 10:30 - 10:55 (B + D days)

__no__ | * P. E. - 2:30 - 3:00 (A + E days) - gym

__yes__ | P. E. - 2:30 - 3:00 (B + D days) - gym

__no__ | P. E. - 2:30 - 3:00 (C day) - West playroom

__no__ | * Art - 10:50 - 11:40 (A2 - day) - art room

__no__ | * Library - Usually "B" day at 11:00 ___ or 1:30 ___

__no__ | * Mrs. Bogan - counselor - 11:25

8:45 | Attendance, Pledge, Song; Announcements, Handwriting -

9:00 | Rotate Reading Groups -

10:00 | Break   10:10

10:30 |

11:00 |

11:40 | 12:00 Lunch

12:45 - Rotate Math Groups

1:30 |

2:30 | P. E.   3:00 - Work Period

47

Lesson Plans

Day __E__   Date _____

Special Times and *Special Area Teachers

__no__   * Music - 10:30 - 10:55 (B + D days)

__yes__ * P. E. - 2:30 - 3:00 (A + E days) - gym

__no__   P. E. - 2:30 - 3:00 (B + D days) - gym

__no__   P. E. - 2:30 - 3:00 (C day) - West playroom

__no__   * Art - 10:50 - 11:40 (A2 - day) - art room

__no__   * Library - Usually "B" day at 11:00 ___ or 1:30 ___

__maybe__ * Mrs. Bogan - counselor - 11:25

8:45	Attendance, Pledge, Song, Announcements, Handwriting -
9:00	Rotate Reading Groups -
10:00	Break 10:10
10:30	
11:00	
11:40	12:00 Lunch
12:45	- Rotate Math Groups
1:30	
2:30	P. E. 3:00 - Work Period

Reading Plans for week of _____

READING GROUPS			
MONDAY:			
Teacher's Edition pp. ___			
Reading Book pp. ___			
Skillpack pp. ___			
Resource Worksheet pp. ___			
TUESDAY:			
Teacher's Edition pp. ___			
Reading Book pp. ___			
Skillpack pp. ___			
Resource Worksheet pp. ___			
WEDNESDAY:			
Teacher's Edition pp. ___			
Reading Book pp. ___			
Skillpack pp. ___			
Resource Worksheet pp. ___			
THURSDAY:			
Teacher's Edition pp. ___			
Reading Book pp. ___			
Skillpack pp. ___			
Resource Worksheet pp. ___			
FRIDAY:			
Teacher's Edition pp. ___			
Reading Book pp. ___			
Skillpack pp. ___			
Resource Worksheet pp. ___			

"A" DAY	"B" DAY	"C" DAY	"D" DAY	"E" DAY
8:25-8:30 Opening Activity	8:25-8:30 Opening Activity	8:25-8:30 Opening Activity	8:25-8:30 Opening Activity	8:25-8:30 Opening Activity
8:30-8:45 Current Events etc.	8:30-8:45 Current Event etc.	8:30-8:45 Current Events etc.	8:30-9:45 Current Events etc.	8:30-8:45 Current Events etc.
8:45-9:35 Reading				
9:35-10:00 P.E.	9:35-10:00 P.E.	9:35-10:00 P.E.	9:35-10:00 P.E.	9:35-10:00 P.E.
10:00-10:15 Break	10:00-10:15 Break	10:00-10:15 Break	10:00-10:15 Break	10:00-10:15 Break
10:15-10:35 Spelling	10:15-10:25	10:15-10:40	10:15-10:25	10:15-10:35
	10:25-10:50 Music		10:25-10:50 Music	
10:35-11:25 Math	10:50-11:25 Math	10:40-11:25 Math	10:50-11:25 Math	10:35-11:25 Math

50

NOON ------------	11:25 - 12:15	------------	Tardy Bell 12:20
12:20-12:40 Read to Class	12:20-12:40 Read to Class	12:20-12:40 Read to Class	12:20-12:40 Read to Class
12:40-1:20 Science 4-W	12:40-1:20 Science 4-W	12:40-1:20 Science 4-W	12:40-1:20 Science 4-W
1:20-2:00 Science 4-R	1:20-2:00 Science 4-R	1:20-2:00 Science 4-R	1:20-2:00
2:00-2:15 Recess	2:00-2:15 Recess	2:00-2:15 Recess	2:00-2:15 Recess
2:15-3:05 Language Arts	2:15-3:05 Language Arts	2:15-3:05 Language Arts	2:15-3:05 Language Arts

Dismissal at 3:10 --------------

MONDAY   "B" Day

9:50   <u>Social Studies</u>

1) Assign: Do <u>open</u> <u>book</u> unit test (pp. 17-18)

.....Will check grade ----> Tuesday

2) Collect/correct/share booklets

10:20   **Break**

10:40   <u>Language Arts</u>   (East Side)

1) Finish limerick ---> Recite

2) "Stopping by words" write & memorize

3) Color patterns ---> put on door
use markers/crayons/or colored pencils

12:05   **Lunch**

12:40   **Square I**

1:10   **Gator Time**

1:30   <u>Math</u>

- Single digit division

- Do worksheet #30 P

- Peer helpers

2:00   <u>Phy. Ed.</u> - **Movement Ed.**

- Trench

- BB relays

- BB skills

2:25   **Finish Math**

3:00   **Dismiss**

ABBREVIATED DAILY SCHEDULE

A.M. Schedule

8:40 Lunch Count
      Calendar
      Pledge
      News
      Sharing

9:00 L.D.
9:00 ESL
9:05 Ch. I

9:10 Explain & Assign
      Seatwork

9:15 "Hotrodders" Reading Group

9:40 "Batmen" Reading Group

10:05 "Readers" Reading Group

10:30 Positive Action   At
      Storytime   Rocker

10:55 P.E.

Reading Plans

 - folders on Reading Table

ESL   = Rath
         Chantha

Ch. I = Nicole
         Peter
         Crystal

L.D. = Josh
         Chad

LESSON PLANS

		SUBJECT 9:05 - 9:50 GRADE ③	SUBJECT 9:50 - 10:15	10:15-10:40 10:35 GRADE	SUBJECT 10:40- 11:40	11:40 - 11:50-12 GR
E **MONDAY**	Pledge, etc.	MATH (All ¾ switch) Correct: Teach: Assign:	SPELLING & HANDWRITING ① Monday 4th Spelling Lesson ___ PRE test (3rd graders go to Johnson)	4th SCIENCE, SOCIAL STUDIES or HEALTH Correct: Teach: Assign:	READING (See plans found with reading manuals) Children move	POSITIVE ACTION Lesson PP —	LUNCH
A **TUESDAY**	Bulletin Announcements,	MATH Correct: Teach: Assign:	SPELLING Write basic list in cursive and/or Write the words in sentences.	MUSIC*	READING	POSITIVE ACTION Lesson — PP —	
B **WEDNESDAY**	Lunch Count,	MATH Correct: Teach: Assign:	HANDWRITING Teach: PP	SCIENCE, SOCIAL STUDIES or HEALTH Correct: Teach: Assign:	READING	POSITIVE ACTION Lesson — PP —	
C **THURSDAY**	Attendance,	MATH Correct: Teach: Assign:	Thursday 4th Spelling Lesson ___. POST test	SCIENCE, SOCIAL STUDIES, or HEALTH Correct: Teach: Assign:	READING	POSITIVE ACTION Lesson — PP —	
D **FRIDAY**	9:00 - 9:05	MATH Correct: Teach: Assign:	HANDWRITING Teach: PP	MUSIC*	READING Quiet Reading R.I.P. Read	SHARING	LUNCH

For the Week Beginning _____, 19 90 _____ M.B.

	12:35-12:50 SUBJECT	12:50 - 1:30	GRADE	1:30-2:00 SUBJECT	2:00-2:25	2:25-3:10 GRADE	SUBJECT	3:10- 3:15
MONDAY	E D.O.L. A Week ___ Literature	LANGUAGE (3rd) Correct: Teach: Assign: (4th goes to Johnson)		SCIENCE, SOC. STUDIES or HEALTH Correct: Teach: Assign: NEWS	P.E.* Mrs. Daly	Art*	(Specialist every other week.)	CLEAN UP Dismiss at bell
TUESDAY	A Library Mrs. Christen 12:35-1:05	Library Book Exchange 1:05-1:30	& Quiet Reading	Sc., S.S., or Health Correct: Teach: NEWS	P.E. See plans for follow up.	Sc., S.S., Health	or cont. Assign:	CLEAN UP Dismiss at bell
WEDNESDAY	B D.O.L. C Week ___ Literature	LANGUAGE Correct: Teach: Assign:		Sc., S.S., or Health Correct: Teach: NEWS	P.E.* Mrs. Daly	Sc., S.S., Health	or cont. Assign:	CLEAN UP Dismiss at bell
THURSDAY	C D.O.L. D Week ___ Literature	LANGUAGE Correct: Teach: Assign:		Sc. S.S. or Health Correct: Teach: NEWS SAVE folders go home	P.E. follow up	Sc., S.S., Health	or cont. Assign:	CLEAN UP Dismiss at bell SAVE folders
FRIDAY	D D.O.L. E Week ___ Literature	LANGUAGE Correct: Teach: Assign		Sc., S.S., or Health NEWS	P.E. Choice Day	Computer		CLEAN UP Dismiss at bell

Reading folders on cart behind you.
Math foldoro on your loft.

DAY E

8:45 - 9:00   **OPENING** - Pledge/song in large area with Gr. 3/4 Calendar,
Discuss folders in groups of 2 or 3 at table while others
color/write pictures/message from board.

9:00 - 10:00 READING & MATH	9:15 - 9:40 MUSIC - GR. 2
9:00 - 9:15 Casey, Sheila, Kim, John (math) (Rud)	John, Jennifer, Kris
9:15 - 9:45 Cassie, Michelle (reading)	Melissa, Casey, Sheila (EA)
9:45 - 10:10 Kim, (Edmark)	
Cassie, Michelle (math)	**9:45 - 10:10 PHYS.ED. - GR. 2**
	Sheila, Kris
	Jennifer (EA)

10:10   SNACK AND BREAK

10:25 - 11:20 READING & MATH	**10:25 - 10:55 PHYS.ED. - GR. 1**
10:25 - 10:45 Kris, Melissa, Jennifer (math)	Cassie, Kim
10:45 - 11:05 John, Jennifer (reading)	Michelle (EA)
11:05 - 11:20 Kris, Melissa (reading)	

11:20   WASH FOR LUNCH

11:28 - 12:25 LUNCH AND OUTSIDE

12:30 - 12:40 REST WITH TAPE OR RECORD   (12:30 - 1:00 E A's lunch)

12:40 - 1:00 POSITIVE ACTION - STORY

1:00 - 1:40 MATH & READING	
1:00 - 1:20 Casey (reading)	
1:20 - 1:40 Kim, Sheila (reading)	**1:40 - 2:00 GROUP SPEECH**
	entire group goes
<u>Jennifer M.</u> for MATH from GR.2	

2:00 - 2:15

2:15 - 2:30   **GROUP ACTIVITIES (math related) EA's break**

2:30 - 2:55 **PERCEPTUAL/PIC ACTIVITIES**	**2:30 - 3:00 PHYS.ED. - GR. 2**
	(Paukert) Casey, John Melissa (EA)

2:55   GET READY FOR BUSES
3:00   DISMISSAL

==

BUS SCHEDULE

# 56 John, Kris	# 38 Jennifer, Cassie (T,TH Tutor)
# 57 Casey (T,W,Th,to GAtor time)	# 30 Michelle
# 68 Melissa # 69 Sheila	Kim to Kids Come First Van

PHYSICAL THERAPY
===

FRIDAY - Jean   (PT assistant)
10:25 Kris

===

OCCUPTATIONAL THERAPY - BILL VISTAD
===

WEDNESDAY & FRIDAY

12:30   Jennifer - John

 1:00   Kris - Casey

 1:30   Cassie

 2:00   Melissa 2 x month

Lesson Plans for reading are in TE (Teacher Editions) in front of the room.	**Monday**	**Tuesday**
	8:30-8:40 Opening	8:30-8:40 Opening

LD -
   Jacob -
   Andy - 9:30-10:00
	READING
	 8:40-9:15 Level 6
	 9:15-9:50 Level 7
	 9:50-10:30 Level 5
		READING

ESL - 2:30 - 3:05
   Thongvanh
   Songly
	9:30-9:55 Music B & E days	

Monivorn	9:35-10:35 Art D days	

Sam
   Phirum
   Youry
	10:35-11:20 Phy. Ed.
	 CREATIVE WRITING
		10:30-10:55
		 CREATIVE WRITING

	10:55-11:20 Phy. Ed.	10:55-11:20 Phy. Ed.
Speech B & D Days Jacob 2:35-2:55	11:20-11:40 Correct Short Shots (DOL)	11:20-11:40 Correct Short Shots (DOL)
	11:42-12:40 Lunch & Recess	LUNCH
- - - - - - - - - - -	12:45-1:00 Sharing	12:45-1:00 Sharing
DOL - (Daily Oral Language)	1:00-1:15 Literature	1:00-1:15 Literature

Phy. Ed. w/Mr.
   A & C days
   D Day - choice day
	1:15-2:00 DAP	DAP

Art w/
   D days (every other
       D day)
	1:15-2:00 Weekly Reader
	 D-days	

	2:00-2:20 Break outside w/Mrs. Rogers	Break
Music w/ B & E days	2:20-3:05 PIC	PIC

PIC - (Primary
      Integrated
      Curriculum)		

	3:05-3:15 Dismissal and Clean-up	Dismissal and Clean-up

Wednesday	Thursday	Friday
8:30-8:40 Opening	8:30-8:40 Opening	8:30-8:40 Opening
READING	READING	READING

10:30-10:55
Mastery Spelling
Basic & Stretch
    Lesson _____
	10:30-10:55
	    Pre-Basic Spelling
	    Lesson_____
		10:30-10:55
		    Pre-Stretch Spelling
		    Lesson_____

10:55-11:20 Phy. Ed.	10:55-11:20 Phy.Ed.	10:55-11:20 Phy. Ed.
11:20-11:40 C.S.S. (DOL)	11:20-11:40 C.S.S. (DOL)	11:20-11:40 C.S.S. (DOL)
LUNCH	LUNCH	LUNCH

12:45-1:00
Positive Action
	12:45-1:00
	    Positive Action
		12:45-1:00
		    Positive Action

1:00-1:15 Literature	Literature	Literature
DAP	DAP	DAP
Break	Break	Break
PIC	PIC	PIC

Dismissal &
    Clean-up
	Dismissal &
	    Clean-up
	
	Pass out weeks papers.
		Dismissal &
		    Clean-up

Grade 1   Room 113
A.M.   8:45 to 11:25

Monday	<u>Opening</u> - Attendance Lunch Count Announcements <u>Reading</u> - Detailed Lessons Plans on Reading Table	<u>Phy. Ed.</u>	<u>Literature</u>	<u>Writing to Read</u> <u>Other</u>
Tuesday	<u>Reading</u> - Detailed Lesson Plans on Reading Table	<u>Phy. Ed.</u>	<u>Literature</u>	<u>Writing to Read</u> <u>Other</u>
Wednesday	<u>Reading</u> - Detailed Lesson Plans on Reading Table	<u>Phy. Ed.</u>	<u>Literature</u>	<u>Writing to Read</u> <u>Other</u>
Thursday	1 <u>Reading</u> - Detailed Lesson Plans on Reading Table	<u>Phy. Ed.</u>	<u>Literature</u>	<u>Writing to Read</u> <u>Other</u>
Friday	<u>Reading</u> - Detailed Lesson Plans on Reading Table	<u>Phy. Ed.</u>	<u>Literature</u>	<u>Writing to Read</u> <u>Other</u>

Grade 1   Room 113
P.M. 12:30 to 3:00

Music	Math	P.I.C. – Social Studies Health/Science	Daily Oral Language	Handwriting
			Language for Daily Use	Other
Music	Math	P.I.C. – Social Studies Health/Science	Daily Oral Language	Handwriting
			Language for Daily Use	Other
Music	Math	P.I.C. – Social Studies Health/Science	Daily Oral Language	Handwriting
			Language for Daily Use	Other
Music	Math	P.I.C. – Social Studies Health/Science	Daily Oral Language	Handwriting
			Language for Daily Use	Other
Music	Math	P.I.C. – Social Studies Health/Science	Daily Oral Language	Handwriting
			Language for Daily Use	Other

61

		Story	Positive Action Lesson_____ Page _____	PIC	DAP
A					
B	Spelling First writing lesson _____ Record grades / Wri- ting	Story	Positive Action Lesson_____ Page_____		
C	Spelling Practice Day	Story	Positive Action Lesson_____ Page_____		
D	Writing	Story	Positive Action Lesson_____ Page_____		
E	Spelling Second writing lesson _____ Record grades / Wri- ting	Story	Show & Tell Rule: To show one thing!	NO PIC TODAY WEEKLY READER DAY	

(This sheet is used to rotate P.M. subject areas Monday-Friday.)

NOTES:

"*The reward of a thing well done is to have done it.*"

Emerson

	Assignment		
E	8:35 - 9:20 Reading	9:25 - 9:50 Music Special Instructor 10 - 10:45 Language	10:45 - 11:25 Math
A	Assignment 8:35 - 9:25 Reading	9:30 - 10:30 Language	10:30 - 11:25 Math
B	Assignment 8:25 - 9:20 Reading	9:30 - 10:30 Language	1030 - 11:25 Math
C	Assignment 8:35 - 9:30 Reading	9:30 - 10:30 Language	10:30 - 11:25 Art Special Instructor every other cycle
D	Assignment 8:35 - 9:20 Reading	9:30 - 10:00 Handwriting 10:00 - 10:25 Music Special Instructor	10:30 - 11:30 Math

Assignment	1:30-1:55 Phy Ed	2:45 - 3:10 Spelling
12:20-12:40 Read + Study	Special Instructor	
12:40 - 1:25 Soc St. (Tennis)	2:00-2:45 Soc. St. (Stender)	
		3:10 Dismissal
Assignment	1:30-1:55 Phy. Ed.	2:45-3:10 Spelling
12:20-12:40 Read + Study	Special Instructor	
12:40 - 1:25 Soc St. (Tennis)	2:00-2:45 Soc. St. (Stender)	
		3:10 Dismissal
Assignment	1:30-1:55 Phy. Ed.	2:45-3:10 Spelling
12:20-12:40 Read + Study		
12:40-1:25 Soc. St. (Tennis)	2:00-2:45 Soc. St. (Stender)	
		3:10 Dismissal
Assignment	1:30-1:55 Phy. Ed.	2:45- 3:10
12:20-12:40 Read + Study	Special Instructor	
12:40-1:25 Soc. St. (Tennis)	2:00-2:45 Soc. St. (Stender)	
		3:10 Dismissal
Assignment	1:30-1:55 Phy. Ed.	2:30-3:10 Computer Lab
12:20-12:40 Read + Study		
12:40-1:25 Language	2:00-2:30	
		3:10 Dismissal

	*B/E =		
	1. Music	=	10:10-10:35
	2. + Action	=	10:20-10:45
	3. Break 1	=	10:05-10:20
	4. Break 2	=	10:35-10:45

Week # _____
Week of: _____

	L/Arts D.O.L. Writing	* P.E.		Spell./Hand.	Math
	9:19-9:35	9:35-10:05	10:10-10:??	10:45-11:15	11:15-11:??
MONDAY				Introduction to Spelling Unit _____ Obj:_____	
TUESDAY				Handwriting	
WEDNESDAY				Study Spelling for Thur. Test	
THURSDAY				Test Spelling	
FRIDAY				Handwriting	

9:00 - 9:10 Attendance, Opening in Pod Area, Announcements . . . . .

11:45 or 11:50 Ready room for lunch . . . . .

NOTES

Portholes

66

		"E" day = Free Choice READING		A = 2-2:30 Library - Choose books B-D = P.I.C. & Coop. Learning E = Ship Meeting & 2:40 Computer Lab F1 = Art* F2 = My Art			
		1:00 - 1:45		2:00 - 3:00			
MONDAY							
TUESDAY							
WEDNESDAY							
THURSDAY	Read to students		Recess				Closure, Clean, Evaluate the day.
FRIDAY	12:45 - 1:00		1:45 - 2:00				3:00 - 3:10 THURSDAY NIGHT = PASS OUT PARENT FOLDERS, TOO!
NOTES							*

NOTES:

"The less one has to do, the less time one find to do it."

Lord Chesterfield

Chapter V - First Day/Week of School

TEACHER PLEASE NOTE: Please be aware that many of the ideas shared by teachers can and do transcend across several grade levels. Be sure to read all grades' suggestions in order to profit from the many other excellent ideas.

INTRODUCTION

Each year I ask, **"How can I get better organized?"** I have organized myself over time and I still ask the same question each year.

This is one of the critical first steps towards a successful year. It is crucial to set objectives and expectations with students right away. That means <u>you</u> need to know most of them as well as possible **before** the students arrive.

Think through the routines you'll want to teach your students. A suggested list is included.

Establish a working rapport. Assess students' desires and needs in terms of academic, socio-emotional, and physical attributes as soon as possible. This will continue throughout the year.

Consider any year-long projects that need to be started early.

Ideas to help you focus on meaningful needs during the first day/week of school will be presented in this chapter.

> *"Time well-spent during the first two weeks of school will buy you all kinds of time the rest of the year."*

> *Steve Milburn (1989)*
> *A Rochester Teacher*

(First Day/Week of School)

Assume nothing! Do a lot of modeling of what you want, with lots of practice of it. Teach for: **1)** classroom management, **2)** procedures, **3)** skills of independence, and anything else you want to happen by design. A starting list of ideas to address follows:

Room rules

Building rules

Attendance taking

Desk organization

Student seating arrangements

Playground safety

Playground equipment

Hall expectations

Where to hang wraps

Bus procedures

Before/after school

Library check out

Getting drinks

Getting and returning
  materials

Independent time use when
  work is finished

How students are to record
  various information

Daily opening exercise
  - pledge
  - calendar
  - announcements
  - song
Closing exercises

How to line up

Pencil sharpening

Lavatory procedures

Lunchroom directions

How to hand in papers,
  money, notes, etc.

Lunch boxes' location

Tour the building - Introduce
  Secretary, Custodian,
  Cook, Crossing guard, etc.

Listening & following directions

Ask them what they need to
  know

Room snacks

Emergency drills

Ready room to leave at
  the end of the day

How to color

Show and tell

Accidents
Rotation of student groups
Clothes storage: hooks/lockers
Birthdays/parties
V.C.R., T.V., and other audio
  visual machines
Computer use
Telephone use

FIRST DAY

Be super organized and overplanned the first day. Walk through the day mentally and visually before the students arrive. Talk slowly so your words of extreme importance are not lost. They will set the directions for the whole year. Having the students come in and sit down immediately at their desk with their name on it will give you the edge on giving directions before action begins. Go step-by-step, building a consistent routine.
(See examples "A" and "A1", pp. 79, 80)

REDUCE ANXIETY

Tour the building, introduce all the key school personnel, and talk about hallway rules. This relieves a lot of anxiety.

FOLLOW THE YARN

Use a yarn ball to lay out a route to be followed by students if it's their first time in the library, or through a set routine. It's like following footprints.

OUTSIDE

Tour the playground. Talk about each piece of playground equipment and safety tips. Point out bus pickup areas, where to line up before school, etc.

NAME TAGS

Make name tags for each student by covering old homecoming buttons with contact paper. Use permanent magic marker to print on the names. Students may keep them at the end of the year. They are big hits with special area teachers, subs, etc. Check with any group that uses buttons for promotions. They invariably have left overs that no one wants.

LEARN NAMES

To help students learn each other's names, play **"Call Ball."** Students sit in a circle and roll the ball to someone. They have to call out the other person's name before the ball is rolled. The teacher plays so that they can include the ones who have not had a turn. Play several days. Make a rule that they cannot roll to the same person twice.

OUTSIDE TOGETHER

Don't rule out playing outside games together. It gives pupils a chance to see each other in a different way, it's fun, and you can informally evaluate sportsmanship and physical skills. Dodgeball, Pom Pom, Kickball, and relays are a few examples.

LEARN THROUGH GAMES

Start to build skills of listening and following directions through fun activities. These are non-threatening for students who do not know you very well, yet. Trust and security must be built in a low-pressure atmosphere, first.

CHART "CAN DO"
Have each student fill in a chart on things they **can** do. You can make up your own chart appropriate to your grade level. Include academic skills, social skills, and practical skills like tying shoes, zipping coats, using a padlock, knowing their address-birthday-telephone number, etc.

DEVELOPING RULES
Have students list rules **they** want. Pare them down into short, workable statements (no more than 3-4 positive "to dos"). Post them in the room for easy reference. Modify them as it becomes appropriate.

ORGANIZING STUDENTS' DESKS
Teach students how to organize their desks. Large books on the bottom, personal items in a box, folder for loose papers, etc. It must be taught. It isn't enough to tell them "Clean up your desk."

"TIME CAPSULE"
Start a **"Time Capsule."** Include feelings, hopes, dreams, and expectations. Don't forget to include **your** thoughts, as well! It is a lot of fun to open it up at the end of the year to have each student read his/hers as a culminating activity. It will be interesting to see the results, not to mention the growth in handwriting skills.

WELCOME NOTE
Prepare a hand-written card for each child and have it on their desk. Perhaps a school house on the front of the card with school name, grade, and their name. A welcome note with a personal touch will acclimate the child just that much faster. **(See example "B", pp. 81, 82)**

SPECIAL SHARING
Have the students bring something from home to share. It gives them a more secure feeling having a connection from home there at school. Keep them on a special table so they don't become a "security blanket."

"Sometimes you need to go slower to be able to

go faster."

Dan Hill
A Rochester Teacher

ASSESS LEVELS

Remember not to compare with or expect the same attention span as your last spring's class. These new students are a year younger. Do simple activities and change them often. Assess levels of abilities with some of these suggestions:

- Fold a sheet of paper into 20 squares (following directions), then write the numerals 1-20 in the squares (check for order, neatness, name, and formation of numerals).

- Draw a picture about something they did this summer (art).

- Write a story (Language Arts skills).

- Read their story (oral, speaking skills).

- Say a word that begins with "A," the next student says one that starts with "B," etc. (alphabet skills).

- Review concept of right and left.

READING SUCCESS

Start the success of reading early by writing down things that are important to individual students. Have them practice reading these short, easy sentences to the class. It gives real meaning and purpose to Language Arts when it is personalized. It will help relieve fears about learning to read.

FIRST WEEK READING

Since most students come to school to learn how to read, be sure to send something home with them the first week that they can read for themselves. Reinforce success in reading early. Have them read to someone at home out loud after they've practiced. **(See example "C", p. 83)**

"WHO GOES HOME NOW"

Make a master list to post on the wall regarding who rides the bus, who walks home, and who is picked up by their parents. This will help you know who is doing what, right, from day to day. You might even pair up a designate partner to shuttle homework back and forth to absent students based on demography.

NOTES:

"The best managers are the teachers who find more time for learning by devoting a great deal of time during the first week of school to teach management expectations."

Carol Cummings (1985)

LEARN NAMES

Give students a tentative weekly class schedule and a class list to follow along with and help learn each other's names. Parents like to see these two items the first day, too.

ICE-BREAKER

Do an ice-breaker activity. Have them mix with each other by filling in a sheet with personal data from other students, such as birthdays in different months, color of hair, eyes, etc. The other students sign by the appropriate category until the paper is complete. **(See example "D", p. 84)**

ART PROJECT "NAME TAGS"

Have an art project with contact paper for name tags for each student's desk. It is to be used for the entire year. Secure to the front of the desk so they last longer and remain in good shape. Perhaps change to cursive versus manuscript and redo them in the middle of the year.

PERSONAL COLLAGE

Have everyone, including yourself, make a personal collage about themselves. When completed, tell the class about it. Perhaps write a short biography on the back. Have old magazines handy for pictures, just in case some are uncomfortable drawing.

POSTER ABOUT YOU

Develop a reusable tagboard poster presentation about yourself. Display it at the beginning of the year. It will let the students know you better and feel more comfortable to share things about themselves. Include pictures of your family, travel, hobbies, etc.

STUDENT'S OWN POSTER

Have the students make **Personal Posters** to hang up for open house in the fall and to help get to know each other sooner. Include the student's picture, family picture, hobby/interest, projections of what they would like to be like when they grow up, etc. Add your own ideas. Include personal information blanks to be filled in, illustrate, and add art work and color.

"MEMORIES"

Start a **Picture Paragraph Project**. Take "slide" pictures throughout the school year of memorable events. Each time a picture is taken, one of the students writes a paragraph about it in the **Picture Paragraph Journal**. At the end of the year, the slides are shown and the paragraphs read by the author. First day at school, good handwriting position, fun times to remember, guest speakers, award presentations, and other memorable events can be relived. This walk down memory lane is fun, positive, and a learning experience.

"PEN PALS"

Establish **"Pen Pals"** with a **"like class"** in a different building. During the last week of school, schedule a picnic to meet, greet, and eat with their year-long pen pals.

QUICK QUES-TIONNAIRES

See examples "E", "F", and "F1" on pp. 85-87 for two quick autobiographical questionnaires. They provide a meaningful language arts assignment while letting you in on some of the students' innermost feelings. They even give you a pretest to look at to decide which English skills to start on first.

AUTOBIOG-RAPHIES

Have students write autobiographies. You'll get to know the students better and they provide the makings of the first student-made bulletin board. Try adding a self-drawn caricature. Write one about yourself. Read them to the class.

"The way of success is not run with seven league boots, but step by step, little by little, bit by bit----with no exceptions allowed."

Sterling Sill

SAVE FROM LAST YEARS

Save last year's weekly/daily schedule to help build the current one. Make masters of the daily ones after a week or so. They can be large enough to be a permanent posting to eliminate writing them over each day.

ROOM THEME

Pick a theme for the room. Try to hook into the latest fad, movie, or T.V. show. The trick is to peg the interest of the students in order to capture their attention early.

"TALK" SESSION

Try starting with a talk session in a circle to find out about feelings and expectations. Discuss students new to the school, curriculum, questions, problems and rules.

BABY PICTURES

Have each student bring in one of their baby pictures. Put them all up on a bulletin board with a number under each. Students have 2-3 days to guess who is who. The person who accurately guesses the most gets a prize. Have each point out their own and tell something about themselves to check the guesses.

PAIR STUDENTS

Pair students up from information gathered from cum folders and first impressions. Pair them with people they don't know very well. Have them discuss topics of "my best friend, and why," "my interest(s) is...," "your choice..." After a period of time ask each student to introduce their partner and share about the topics that they have been discussing.

LISTENING SKILL

Play **"SPARKLE."** Spell one word going through the students one letter at a time. When the word is spelled, the next student says **"SPARKLE."** The next student starts to spell the same word, giving the first letter, etc. Teamwork, review of how to spell a word, and listening skills are built early in the year. When everyone has had a turn, introduce a different word.

CAMP OUT

Organize a 3-day camping trip as soon as possible. This is an opportunity to really get to know each other. Hold lots of circle talks, do problem solving, and establish guidelines and attitudes for the year. Involve more than one classroom for twice the advantage both in shared experiences and expenses.

DEVELOPING RULE(S)

For a feeling of student cooperation, interaction, and ownership involving classroom rules, put students into small groups. Have them brainstorm all the rules they would like for their class. Post all of these papers on the walls. Talk about how hard it would be to memorize all of them. Ask students how to simplify these to fewer in number. Key in on words like "respect," "others," "rights," etc. Ask how one rule can fit all? Come up with some statement like: "Always respect the rights of others." Discuss the statement to see if it will cover all the rules on the papers, and work for all types of situations. When all agree, it becomes the class rule for the year. Another possibility might be: "You can do anything you want to as long as you don't hinder anyone else's learning or your own."

SEATING ARRANGEMENT

Have the students do their own seating arrangement by filling out a form. A group of 3-4 students will complete the seating from the forms. It saves you time, gives the small group a unique problem to solve, and the students will feel more ownership in the room. **(See example "G", p. 88)**

"A goal is a dream with a deadline."

Steve Smith
Amdahl Corporation

DEVELOP MASTER LIST

Keep a detailed master list of first day/week activities, schedule, and routines to teach. Reuse this same list each year, revising as necessary.
(See examples "H", "I", "I1", and "J", pp. 89-92)

START OF THE YEAR FOLDER

Establish a **"Beginning of the Year Folder."** Keep masters of the first few week's papers to run off, a detailed list/lesson plan for the first day or two (to be revised and refined each year), and inspirational thoughts to review each new school year. Include blank forms for classlist, weekly/daily schedules, lesson plan pages, seating chart, spelling test blanks, etc.

ROUTINES

Assume nothing! Routines are the number one priority, curriculum is secondary for the first two weeks. Modeling and practicing will prove that you think your expectations are important enough to follow through on the rest of the year.

SHARING

Hand out 3 M & Ms to each student. They can only eat them after sharing about a topic.
> Red = tell one fun thing you did this summer.
> Yellow = tell one thing you really like about school.
> Brown = tell one thing you feel you're good at.

PRETESTING

After students have settled in during the first week of school, start individual assessments (pretesting) of each child in several areas. This is important due to the fact that many children's skills have increased over the summer and some have not retained what they previously learned. This is not reflected in the end-of-year reports. If you zero in on where they really are, versus what their records indicate, you can save time by not having to reteach later or teaching what they already know.

COOPERATIVE GROUPS

Start to develop **"Cooperative Learning Groups"** right away. Run several **"trust activities"** covering expectations for the year. Gather the data and share your feelings, too. Maybe they could invent a handshake for just their group.

TEACHING EXPECTATIONS

Practice makes permanent. Use the attitude of teaching expectations; not expecting things to have already been taught or remembered.

HAND-OUT FOR PARENTS

Design a pamphlet to hand out on meet-the-teacher day or at your first open house. New parents moving in during the year will also appreciate knowing they are welcome and what the skeleton coverages will be. It may be designed on the computer and folded into a book.
(See example "K", p. 93)

POSITIVE ACTION

A kit is available entitled **Positive Action**. It is filled with enough 20 minute lessons to cover each day of the school year. It is an excellent way to start right out with a positive environment from day/week one. The address is:

Positive Action
321 Eastland Drive
P.O. Box 2347
Twin Falls, ID 83301

(208) 733-1328

SIGN-UP

Set out a sign-up list for volunteers during the first "Meet the Teacher" day. Meet once with all the volunteers to establish your ground-rule expectations. This meeting should be at the start of the year. Go over the what and how of things clearly. Everyone hears the same thing and has a chance to decline if they wish.

"Good, better, Best.
Never let it rest.
Make the good better,
And the better Best."

Anonymous

FIRST DAY OF THE WEEK

"A"   DAY

Get attendance sheet.

- Markers to label   - Ready P.M. slides
- Put schedule on board - Follow directions sheet
- Put date on board   - Book to read to students
- Get stretch lists Unit 1 - + worksheet   graph

8:45   **Meet outside**

9:00   All to seats - belongings on floor
          Attendance and lunch count
              - say hot or cold and favorite hobby
                Model: "cold and motorcycling"

9:15   **Welcome aboard**   **New ship**   **new crew**
              - Sea of learning   - grade 2 - grade 4
              - Islands of education   - Thought is taught here

          * **Introduce myself** background & family

          Tour Ship: Their agenda 1st

                  - Portholes
                  - Bathroom ships
                  - Duty Board
                  - Plank/throttle/4 Room Rules
                  - To Do's Talbe
                  - Tubs - in cupboards
                  - Shells
                  - Captain's Cabin (2 at a time)
                                     (Telephone by permission)
                  - Sink Pirate Ship
                  - 2 Cabinets....**YOURS** and **MINE**
                  - Questions ?

9:25   **Ready P.E.** Warm up kickball: 2 teams each kick once

9:35   **Out**   Outside shoes ? Use our door
                     Bathroom rules
                     Hall noise -- whisper or "0".

10:05   **Bathroom Break**
              Drinks - quiet 1st!

              * Snack = nutritious
In   * Lunch sacks to box (or lockers A.M.)
seats   * Desks arranged
  to   * Tubs - Books = Note #'s + toys!
explain   * Glue
              * Scissors
              * Sharpen (2 only) pencils
                Label everything!

10:30   **To lockers:** Assign #'s

79

10:40   Enough talk, let's speed up
        <u>spelling</u> notebooks: Pencil and notebooks.

M	W	Th	F
Pre test	study	test	retakes
Basic	+ Mr. Bailey, Captain		at breaks
	+ Miss Connor, Co-captain		

Label notebooks as <u>Spelling</u> + <u>name</u>.
\# 1-5 L of margin continue through 20.
  on transparency as we go...
* TO DO: (on board) Study for Spelling test Thursday!

11:25   <u>Math</u> + / - **Typewriter**

11:40   **Ready Lunch**
        Straighten room(quick & quiet)
        Ball sign out?
        Lunch bags from box
        Alphabetical hot lunch line on R
        <u>Never</u> to room w/o pass........Orange sheet for rules
        <u>Right</u> outside.................   "   "   "   "
        <u>In</u> <u>seats</u> at 12:55!...........   "   "   "   "

11:50   **To lunch**

 PUT   SCHEDULE   ON   BOARD

12:45   **Drinks/attendance**
        I read to them: <u>Aesop's Fables</u>
                     <u>Norway Fairy Tales</u>
                     <u>Notes in a Bottle</u>

 1:00   **Reading   OBJ: Rdg. skills & art skills**
        Reason: Show me <u>your</u> <u>best</u>. + Porthole??
        Following directions sheets.   <u>F.T.G.</u>
        I assign by Rdg. level
        * Call up all 7's, 6's, 5's

 1:45   **Recess.....Whistle * 2 blasts = line up fast**
        Picture as a group ....   I hand out balls

 2:00   **Slide Show presentation**
        1. Work; learn; have fun   2. ?'s afternoon

 2:20   **Writing Folders + Study Pd. Rules**
        Ship's log   Sea Date Sept. 4, 1990
        TO DO'S (Math/Rd.Sheets)   <u>Show</u> <u>my</u> <u>diary</u>...

 2:55   **Collect Folders**

 3:00   **Evaluate Day - Throttle**
        Clean floor and desks
        TO DO's for homework + emergency slips
        ? / Comments
        Fish Book + Riddle
        Blue Bus Rules Sheet

Hi!

I am so happy that you are in my class. We will have fun getting to know each other and learning many things. Together we will make this a great year in first grade.

Love,

Mrs.

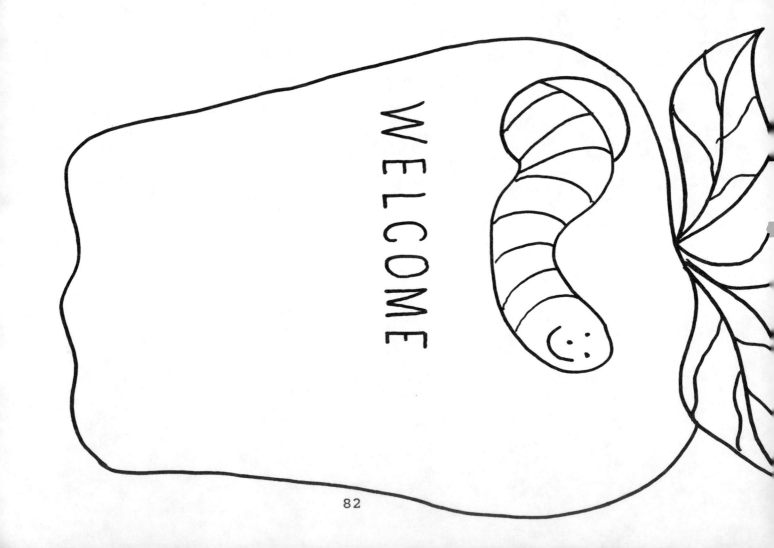

WELCOME

My Red Book

r e d

R e d

The (ball) is red

are

_____

- - - - - - - - - -

_____

I like red.

Word Matching

red   Red

Red   red

red   red

Red   Red

red

Find A Person Who ....

is female	has culy hair	is taller than you	likes to read
has a 10-speed bike	likes to ski	is wearing purple	likes pizza
has brown eyes	is the same height as you	is male	walks to school
has a pet	has blonde hair	is shorter than you	is older than 20

NAME_____

DATE_____

1.   Today I feel _____

2.   When I have to read, I _____

3.   To be grown up _____

4.   I wish my parents knew _____

5.   School is _____

6.   I feel bad when _____

7.   I wish teachers _____

8.   I wish my mother _____

9.   To me, books _____

10.   I would rather read than _____

11.   To me, homework _____

12.   I hope I will never _____

13.   I wish people would not _____

14.   When I finish high school _____

15.   I am afraid _____

16.   When I take my report card home _____

17.   I am at my best when _____

18.   Most brothers and sisters _____

19.   I wish _____

20.   When I read aloud _____

21.   I would read more if _____

22.   I look forward to _____

23.   I often worry about _____

24.   I wish I could _____

25.   I would like to be _____

26.   I like to read when _____

All About Me....

My name: _____

My teacher: _____

Three things I do well:_____

_____

_____

Three things I would like to learn this year: _____

_____

_____

My best subject:_____

The subject I need the most help with:_____

My favorite hobby/sport is:_____

Things I do outside of school:_____

_____

_____

Lesson(s) I take outside of school:_____

_____

My three best friends are:_____

_____

_____

A picture of my family:

One thing I am proud of:_____

_____

Two things I like to do with others:_____

_____

_____

MY NAME IS: _____

We will give you **ONE** of these.

1. One boy I would like to sit with is: _____

2. One girl I would like to sit with is: _____

3. One table I would like to sit at is: _____

_____

MY NAME IS: _____

We will give you **ONE** of these.

1. One boy I would like to sit with is: _____

2. One girl I would like to sit with is: _____

3. One table I would like to sit at is: _____

_____

MY NAME IS: _____

We will give you **ONE** of these.

1. One boy I would like to sit with is: _____

2. One girl I would like to sit with is: _____

3. One table I would like to sit at is: _____

_____

MY NAME IS: _____

We will give you **ONE** of these.

1. One boy I would like to sit with is: _____

2. One girl I would like to sit with is: _____

3. One table I would like to sit at is: _____

_____

FIRST DAY REMINDERS......

_____ AALC

_____ Welcome!

_____ Introduce myself   _____ Introduce Don

_____ * Seating arrangement - desks/chairs (size)

_____ * Schedule: switching
        - noon-hour
        - today's schedule

_____ Around-the-room
        - hall hooks
        - textbook cabinet
        - gum
        - bathroom privileges & drinks & sharpen pencil
        - Fire exits - last one out - Map on Wall

_____ News articles

_____ Name plates & tags   _____ Room cleanup

_____ Rules - as necessary   _____ Buses

- OTHER MISCELLANEOUS -

1) **Evacuation map is on wall by light switch.**

2) **Room Rules:** may set up your own rules for the day!

3) **Class procedures**
   a) Attendance sheet put out on door by 8:50 am and 12:35 pm
      (includes lunch count)
   b) Pick up daily bulletin in office - share "students"
      section with class. Save for me.
   c) Clipboard on wall to be used <u>in lunch line</u> for hot
      lunchers.
   d) I usually start out day with a <u>news discussion</u> (some may
      have articles to share).
   e. Telephone permission slips, detention slips, noon-hour
      permission slips are in top-right desk drawer.

- FILLER (extra time) SUGGESTIONS -

1) Weekly Reader (look on top of file cabinet)
2) Any creative writing assignment
3) Language "short-shots"
4) Math extra credit sheets (see file marked "Math")
5) Any of your own that you may have brought along

FIRST DAY REMINDERS

GYM TIMES

BATHROOMS - The children may leave the room one boy and girl at a time.

BUSES - AM   Take the students to the front door. The children are able to find their buses by themselves. May need some help with taxis and vans.

- PM   All the students go to the gym. Please help the other teachers get the students to their correct buses.

1. You ususally will find the materials you need on my desk or in the green buckets behind my desk. Music and Physical Education equipment is found under the flannel board.

2. I understand it's not always possible to complete everything in the plans. You don't have to follow the schedule if you think the lessons may work better in another order.

3. Please make sure windows are closed at the end of the day.

4. Please make your comments on the following pages. = Thank You For Coming! Have a Good Day!

.....Part missing

F. Calendar - The helper places the circle around the correct numeral and tells the class the month and day (with help). The helper then points to each numeral and the class counts up to the day's date.

G. Weather Chart - The same helper puts up the weather hands and we discuss the weather. We then sing the morning or afternoon greeting. Children know the song, but you can find it on the next pages.

H. Pledge and Sing America

I. V.I.P. (Very Important Person) - List of names is found on the wall above the record player. The first day of the week the V.I.P. brings in items. He/she tells and shows the class the items. The items are put up on the V.I.P. board. The items are sent home on the last day of the week.

J. Birthdays - The birthday hats, boxes and jack-in-the-boxes are found in the top drawer in the closet by my desk. The jack-in-the-box jumps out on the child's birthday. Put on birthday hat and sing song. If child brings treat, he/she can have it when you sing.

K. Sharing Bags - The schedule for the sharing bags is found on the wall above the record player. The assigned students take the sharing bags home the first day of the week and return it with the sharing item the end of the week. The student gives the clues to the class and they try to guess what is in the bag. The student tells what is special about the sharing item, after the students have guessed what it is. The sharing item is sent home in their backpack the same day.

Library - Every TUESDAY

AM -

PM -

Library Charts: They are found behind the flannel board. When students return their books, they put in the library card and take out the date due card. They put them in the library book box. The teacher is responsible for the students in the library. The students are to be "quiet." They are to pick out a book, bring it to the table and sign it out. They cannot get a new book if they did not return the old one.

Items Covered by One Teacher During the
First Week of School

- Song
- Pledge
- Attendance
- Lunch count
- Bulletin
- Put things away, collect money, paint sheets, letters, etc.
   (kleenex)
- Tell what each is for - calendar, weather, etc.
- Name tags
- Collect extra pins
- Helpers' jobs
- Sharing days - overhead
- Bathroom passes
- Room policies/rules
- Balls, etc. go around room and show
- Walk around building
- Playground safety rules
- Room constitution

- Break/restroom

- Butterflies - metamorphis
   change - felt board
- Get ready for lunch
* Review playground rules - When to come in (bell - back door)
- Wash hands
- Lunch
- Story - Little Engine
- Review - One Potato Two Wards

- Listener Rules
- Video - sharing: Name brothers & sisters
                    Favorite thing to do, hobbies, summer?
- Break
- Fun sheets
- School Bus Safety Rules
- Prepare for dismissal
- Check bus numbers
- Dismiss

GREETINGS AND WELCOME ABOARD CAPTAIN BAILEY'S U.S.S. FRIENDSHIP

--Fold here--

--Fold here--

BASIC GOALS THIS YEAR:
1. Math
        Review + and - (with renaming)
        Teach x and - (0-5s minimum)
2. Reading skills furthered through
        Basal Textbook
        Phonics
        Library Reading
        Student Writing Folders
3. Language Arts
        Spelling Units & Personalized Lists
        Cursive Handwriting
            Review small letters
            Teach capital letters
        Sentences and Paragraphs
        Dictionary Skills
        Speaking Skills and Grammar
        Creative Writings
4. PIC (Primary Integrated Curriculum)
        Measurement, Telling Time, Energy
        and Forces, Astronomy, Plants
        Graphing, Dental Unit, Nutrition,
        Family Life, Drugs, Map Skills,
        Norway, Egypt, etc.
5. Computer Technology
6. Cooperative Learning
7. Thinking Skills
8. FURTHER RESPONSIBILITY

9. To have fun learning   93

HAVE A SAFE AND HAPPY LEARNING VOYAGE

LESSON PLANS For **Week Beginning** _____ 19___ School _____, Room _____
or
Week of Year _____ Instructor _____ Grade _____

	SUBJECT	SUBJECT	SUBJECT
M O N D A Y	**Assignment**		

T U E S D A Y
 5
 A
	Assignment
	
	 8:40-9:00
	 - Opening, calendar
	 - supplies in buckets
	    - care
	
	 - Pattern clapping
	
	 9:00 - Assembly
		9:20 - Playground Safety
		    - Slide Hill
		    - Swings
		    - Monkey Bars
		
		 9:30 - Color Song
		
		    - Bathroom Rules
		
		 9:45 - Bathroom Break
			10:00-10:30
			    - P.E. Outside
			
			 10:30 - Read - Good
			           Listening Rules
			       Bernstain Bears
			        Go to School
			 Lunch readiness
			
			 10:50-11:35 - Art
			      Self Portraits

W E D N E S D A Y
 6
 B
	Assignment
	 8:40-9:00
	 - Opening, calendar
	 - Finish Bears & Too
	   Much Vacation
	
	 9-9:35 - Self Portrait
	
	 9:35-10:00 - Music
	     Mrs. Reynolds
		10:00-10:20 - Bathroom
		     Tour School
		
		 10:20-10:40 - Handwriting
		          Sample
		
		 10:45-11:05 - P.E.
		        Solheim
		   Safety on playground
			11:05 - Bernstains Forget
			      Manners
			
			 11:20-11:40 - Lunch
			     Readiness Procedures
			
			 11:45-12:25 - Lunch

T H U R S D A Y
 7
 C
	Assignment
	 8:40-8:50 - Opening
	
	 8:50-9:35 -
	 - Brainstorm s words
	 - Sketch
	 - Students make 8
	   sheets, pick 4 words
	   and sketch
	 9:35-10:00 - Music
	     Mrs. Reynolds
		10:00-10:20 - Bathroom &
		        Outside
		 10:20-10:30 - Snack
		 10:30-11:00 - Sunshades
		
		 11:00-11:15 - Positive
		     Action Lesson
			11:15-11:30 - Story
			
			 11:30-11:40 - Lunch
			      readiness

F R I D A Y
 8
 D
	Assignment
	 8:40-8:50 - Opening
	 8:50 - Film
	 9:30 - Rumpelstiltskin
	   - Sequencing Chart
	 9:30 - Sponge painting
	 10:15 -
		10:15-10:40 - Bathroom
		     Eat watermelon
		     Save seeds
		
		 10:40-11:05 - P.E.w/Roger
		
		 11:05
			11:30 - Lunch readiness
			
			 11:40 - Lunch

LESSON PLANS For Week Beginning _____ 19____ **School** _____ , **Room** _____
                                                                                                    or
           Week of Year _____ Instructor _____ , **Grade** _____

SUBJECT	SUBJECT	SUBJECT

11:15 - Lunch readiness
11:45 - Rules & procedures
    - wash - line up
      alphabetically
12:25-12:45 - Quiet Time
12:45-1:15 - DAP Ruels
	1:15-1:45 - Film
	    Stop, Look & Think
	    Bus Safety Rules
	1:45-2:00 - Recess
	2:00-2:30 - FS
	    Piglet - New Kid In
	      School	

12:25-12:45 - Quiet Time/
      Bathroom
Emergency situation if
teacher out of room
12:45-1:15 - DAP Rules
    - DAPPY BOOK
    - Draw DAPPY
1:15-1:45 - Watercolor
    care of paints
 	
TS - Citizenship at School
	1:45-2:00 - Break
	2:00-2:30 - Films
	    Curious George Rides Bike
	    Children In Autumn
	2:30-3:00 - Author Study
	    Read -	

12:25-12:45 - Quiet Time/
      Bathroom
12:45-1:15 - DAP - Lost &
      Found
    - Intro. bags
    - Review
    - DAPPY THOUGHTS
1:15-1:45 - Film
    Beginning Responsbility
	2:00-2:30 - Handwriting
	2:30-3:00 - Author Study
	    Closure	

12:25-12:45 - Quiet Time
      Bathroom
12:45-1:00 - Glue seeds
    & rins on watermelon
Safety scissors
1:00-1:30 - DAP
1:30-1:45 - Film
	1:45-2:00 - Outside break
	2:00-2:30 - Film
	    Green Eggs & Ham
	    Ant & Grasshopper
	2:30-3:00 - Author Study
	    Closure	

Subject
    Text
    Time

WEEK OF

NOTES

(M) Marietta

Put away supplies
Things to discuss:
Rules-room, hall, playground, lunch, etc.
When to sharpen pencils, get drinks, bathroom
Breaktime, care of materials, etc.

Attendance/lunch count
Discuss rules and choose helpers, calendar
DOL lesson
9:50 - 10:20 P.E. outdoor play on equipment
Make work folder
A.   Activity sheet   Lunch 11:45

Attendance/lunch count (M)
September Calendar   (M) Observe
Handwriting lesson   * 10:45 - 11:10 Music
* 9:50 - 10:20 P.E. (M) Observe
Review dolch words (* both of us)
B.   Activity Sheet   Lunch 11:45

Attendance/lunch count   (M) Observe
DOL lesson   * Marlys 9:20 - 9:50
Review dolch words
Activity sheet
C.   9:50 - 10:20 P.E. Follow-up (M)
                                  Lunch 11:45

Attendance/lunch count
Sharing time   * 10:45 - 11:10 Music
Handwiring lesson
Review dolch words   * Marlys 9:20 - 9:50
Personal reading   Meet your classmates...
D.   * 9:50 - 10:20 P.E.   Lunch 11:45

Attendance
Read to class   12:45 - 1:00   Story: My First Day...
Positive Action   1:00 - 1:30   Unit 1.
Math Inventory test   (M) Checked
* Art 1:50 - 2:40 (in classroom)   (Marietta)
Intro. bulletin board "Beary Special Readers" & actitivy

Attendance
Read to class
Positive Action
Math intro. workbook pgs. 1-4, practice sheet   Break: 2:15 - 2:30
Safety lesson
Bus rules, Poster, Story - Luck Bus - Boyer

Attendance
Read to class
Positive Action
Math pgs. 5-6   Break: 2:15 - 2:30 (rain)
Activity meet the class...   (Marietta)

Attendance   4-0032-02 BEG. RESP.: TAKING CARE OF THINGS YOU SHARE
Read to class
Math pgs. 7-8   Break: 2:15 - 2:30
Safety   Review - writing activity, first draft   (Marietta)
1:45 - 2:15 Brainstorm, go over rules
   Clean desks   Weekly Reader

The Welcome Back to School Book

by Jeri Carrol, Donna Beneredge and Diane McCane

TABLE OF CONTENTS

Reference: GOOD APPLE, INC.
Box 299
Carthage, IL 62321-0299

ISBN No. 0-86653-383-4

Chapter VI - Last Day/Week of School

INTRODUCTION

It is an exciting time of the year. A lot of time and work has been invested. Finish strong by maintaining a meaningful, high-interest learning environment.

Schedule changes are a given. Record keeping, assessments, closures, special projects, room maintenance, and good-byes need to be planned.

The following items are presented for your consideration.

"This time, like all times, is a very good one, if we but know what to do with it."

Ralph Waldo Emerson

NOTES:

"*You don't have **to be** the Best, but you do have to do your Best.*"

Zig Ziglar

THEME FOR A DAY   If all curriculums are completed, go for an extra theme for a day. For example, "Peanuts." Research smell, taste, texture, uses, art, how they grow, etc. Think about it to the "nth degree." Additional ideas: tasting party, how a pencil is made, and what makes a raisin.

BRAINSTORM THE YEAR   Ask the students to think of all of the things the class did this year. List their ideas on the chalkboards. Write small. Use this review further by having the students write a letter to you entitled "What I Want You to Remember Me By." Put a picture of the student with each and make yourself a scrapbook of the year to refer back to. Think of other Language Arts activities to use the list for.

AWARDS   Plan an awards ceremony. All kinds of awards for all types of things and areas (academic, social, etc.). Attendance, subject area accomplishments, most improved in _____, sports, etc. (limited only by your creativity). Share and talk about each one. Make sure each child gets one.

SPLIT ROOMS   Split two rooms up by dividing and pairing up students. It will give you a fresh class, partners to experience cooperation with, and the students will have a different teacher to interact with. Switch classes after a week so everyone gets a turn in the opposite room.

OUTSIDE   Try taking work outside. It is special to have the privilege of working in the fresh, spring air and sunshine.

STUDENT "TEACH"   Have students teach the class about something you have already covered during the year. They get a chance to plan a lesson and see how it feels to be the teacher. It is a good review for everyone.

SUMMER LIST   Make a list of summer activities and take it home. Have students construct a paper chain as they do an activity each day, putting one completion on each link. Return them to school, in the fall, for a prize and link all the chains together.

NOTES:

"*A lost inch of gold may be found; a lost inch of time, never.*"

Proverb

EXCHANGE CLASSES

Have a cooperative teaching day. Exchange classes with other teachers and do a special activity with your "new class." Rotate the classes every 45 minutes or so. Include special area teachers if possible, decreasing the number of each group. Give each student a copy of the schedule and a list of any materials they'll need to bring. It is a great refresher from the usual routine.

YEAR'S PICTURES/ PARAGRAPHS

Start a **Picture Paragraph Project** at the beginning of the year. Take slide pictures throughout the year of memorable events. Each time a picture is taken, one of the students writes a paragraph about it in the **Picture Paragraph Journal**. At the end of the year the slides are shown and the paragraphs read. This walk down memory lane is fun, positive, and a learning experience.

REVIEW PICTURES

After taking pictures throughout the year of different students and different activities, take time to review the pictures and let the appropriate students take them home as mementos. Each student should get at least one.

BOOKLET

Take a black and white picture print of each child and yourself. Glue each at the top of a sheet of white paper. Students write their final draft of **"Most Memorable Events of 19 __"** below the picture. Run enough copies of each student to make a booklet for each. Make covers and take time to write short notes to each other in the yearbooks. Word processing on computers may be integrated with this if you wish.

LETTERS TO NEXT YEAR'S CLASS

Have outgoing students write letters to next year's class. They can leave a legacy with this language arts project. Put them up as a bulletin board for next fall. Encourage them to tell of the pitfalls, things to remember, fun times, things they learned, and things they wish that they could forget. Another writing activity is to write what a visitor may have seen anytime during the year.

AUTOGRAPHS

Have students make up small autograph books. All students write their names and a short message in each of the others' books. Discuss appropriateness and feelings.

THREE-DAY ACTIVITY

All of one grade level conducts a three-day "Points Accumulation Project" during the last week of school. Students use the first two days working for points. They work independently on review packets, record their own self-corrected scores, and use the points as money for an auction on the third day. Each student brings in a "white elephant" gift from home wrapped in newspaper or paper sack. These are auctioned off for the points they earned on the review packets. It is fun, productive, and gives the teacher a little extra time to prepare for the end of the year requirements. The packets are used year after year.

Handwriting review page	Math worksheets
Spelling review test	Silent reading
Encyclopedia research	Creative writing
Poetry with illustration	Alphabetizing
Dictionary work	Crosswords
Word game worksheets	Art
Map work	Your choice.........

Involve parents, media specialists, and special area teachers. **(See examples "A", "A"1", and "A2", pp. 111-113)**

"WORK FOR BUCKS"

The last weeks of school are difficult for students to focus on their learning. Start a project called: **"Work for Bucks."** Reproduce fake dollars called **"bucks."** Students are rewarded for doing well in any area you wish. Students bring "white elephant" gifts to school, wrap them up, and marked for girls or boys. The day before school is out have an auction and bid for the wrapped gifts. Have students write their names on the back of the bucks if they want them back after the auction to play with or keep as a memento. **(See example "B" and "B1", pp. 114, 115)**

FUN THINGS   To keep students on task, try these short-term, **fun tricks**:

<u>Dot-to-dot:</u> Find a challenging dot-to-dot in a coloring book. Run a copy for each child. Give a student permission to fill in another dot whenever you see something positive. Students who complete their dot-to-dot first win a prize.

<u>Bingo:</u> At the start of the day, pass out Bingo cards. Call numbers throughout the day when the whole class is working together well. Bingo winners receive a prize of some kind.

<u>Ice-cream:</u> Make homemade ice cream. While doing this outside project, the class can also discuss the scientific concepts. It also makes a great snack on a hot day.

CHORAL READING   Try some choral reading. It is a real motivator. The reading teacher specialist might be able to help. Perhaps present it to other classes and/or parents.

BOOK OF RECORDS   Do a <u>Class World Book of Records</u>; a spin-off of the <u>Guiness World Book of Records</u>. Brainstorm different academic and social categories and everyone tries to win. Hold the events, make books, and use them as autograph type yearbooks.

"PEN PALS" PICNIC   At the beginning of the year, establish **"Pen Pals"** with a "like class" in a different building. During the last week of school schedule a picnic to meet, greet, and eat with their year-long pen pals.

PAPER QUILTS   Here's a simple and memorable way to celebrate the year you and your students have shared. This is a year-end project called **PAPER QUILTS**. Have students draw a 1/2 inch border around the sides of white paper. This is where the "squares" will be joined. Then have them draw a favorite or memorable event that took place during the school year. On the back, they write a short explanation of the event they chose. Present, read, and arrange them (chronologically?). Glue onto heavy cardboard and cover borders with black construction paper strips. If you're really ambitious, make it out of real cloth and use crayon-transfer. Designs are colored on sandpaper and ironed on. Hang in the room for next year's class to preview.

"You never know when a moment and a few sincere words can have an impact on a life."

Zig Ziglar

PAPERBACKS

If your library closes early for inventory, be prepared. Keep a supply of unseen paperback books to bring out so that your reading program can continue. Do a newspaper unit of current events.

BULLETIN BOARD

Do a bulletin board of this year's activities for next year's students. Cover it with newspaper to preserve over the summer. Have student helpers sign their names.

PERSONAL PROFILES

<u>**Personal Profiles:**</u> Each student writes a descriptive paragraph or ten descriptive sentences about themselves or a classmate. These personal profiles are then collected and a reader reads them aloud omitting any names. Save the "easy" clues for the last. Alternative ideas: Animals, Famous People, Books, Countries, Foods, or Activities.

"THANK YOU NOTES"

Students write Happy-o-Grams and Thank You notes to teachers P.T.S.A., office personnel, supervisors, etc. Combine the writing curriculum with a practical, high interest project that will make students feel good about themselves.

CLEAN-UP HUNT

Have a class **clean-up treasure hunt**. Divide students into teams of 3 or 4. Write clues on paper and hide them around the room, making several clues for each group. Clues are earned by cleaning up an area. Example: Clue 1 = Take down the math bulletin board, check with teacher, go to Brooke's chair for Clue 2.

"CHART YOUR COURSE"

"CHART YOUR COURSE" There's buried treasure on Discovery Island. Your students have to draw treasure maps and write the direction to help their classmates find the booty or destination. Allow student pairs to choose a real location on the school grounds, like the cafeteria, and write steps for getting there. As one classmate paces off the steps to where "X" marks the spot, the other takes notes. Back in the classroom, they draw their map and exchange it with another pair of students. See if kids can guess the destinations by reading the directions and studying the maps.

"MAD LIBS"

A fun filler is to write **"Mad Libs."** These are stories in which you have the students give a verb, noun, adjective, or adverb to fill in the blanks without knowing the text of the real story. Students will enjoy hearing the crazy, mixed up story.

(Last Day/Week of School)

GUESSING COST   One interest activity to try is having the students guess the prices of everyday items at the 1930's cost. Find an old Sears catalog and compare.

"DARE DAY"   Have a **"Super, Sloppy, Double-Dare Day."** Everyone dresses up in old clothes that cannot be ruined, and go outside. Develop questions on 3 x 5 cards from the year's work. Use curriculum guides or teacher editions to pull questions from. If a student misses a question, they must take a challenge such as sing a song, stand on head, catch a water balloon, catch a jello ball, etc. Fun and review mesh (mess) together.

"TIME CAPSULE"
At the beginning of school, start a **"Time Capsule."** Include feelings, hopes, dreams, and expectations. Now is the time to open it up and read what was written to compare results. Don't forget to include your thoughts, as well!

SCRAP BOOK
Start a scrapbook collection for each child at the beginning of the year. Keep stressing it throughout the year. Put everything together and bind it as a souvenir of the year. Inclusions might be: Happy-o-Grams, samples of paperwork, awards, art work, story writing, weekly journal paragraphs, and their choice of "notables."

FAVORITE UNIT
Save one of your favorite units to teach last. Do not stop teaching. It is counter productive to count down days to the end of school. Students will live up to ----- or down to ----- your expectations.

HIGH INTEREST UNIT
Plan a special unit of high interest. For example, hatching eggs into chicks. Include recording, reading, graphing, writing, math, art, etc.

"BIRTHDAY BASH"
Celebrate all the summer and new students' birthdays during the last week of school. Call it a **"Birthday Bash."**

"SUMMER CAN DOS"
Hold a discussion and write down things students can do for themselves during the summer. Have each copy it and take it home for later reference.

MULTI-AGE ACTIVITIES
Multi-age activities are a perfect way to spend some profitable hours during the month of May and June. Have Big friend-Little friend match-ups. Take an end-of-year fun trip together.

* Check out the fast food or other businesses that are close to your school. Many will offer a special deal for school groups.

* Take a nature or litter walk with a check-off sheet: similar to a scavenger hunt.

* Write a letter to your friend and send them during the summer (All kids love mail.) Many PTAs will provide stamps.

Continued.....

* Read to another student outside on the grass. Share a treat or sit together at a school program.

* Adopt an incoming kindergartner. Write them a welcome letter to send in August, and then plan a follow-up visit the 1st week of school next fall.

LAST DAY WALK

On the last day of school walk the students to a fast food place and eat lunch. The walk uses up some of the excess student energy. Maybe just an afternoon ice cream treat. Call ahead. Many times you will get a discount price.

LAST DAY CLEAN UP

Do not put anything in the room away until the last day. The students can all help at their ability level. Cleaning can be a learning experience.

TIME TO REFLECT

The last week of school is a time to be together. Plan it out to include a time to reflect and remember the year's experiences. Solidify all the strengths, growths, enjoyments, and set direction for the future.

POINTS ACCUMULATION PROJECT

(<u>STUDENT TALLY SHEET</u>)

FIRST & <u>LAST</u> NAME:_____

** ALWAYS BRING:

    1. Pencil(s) with eraser! and crayons

    2. Clean notebook paper (lots) <u>in a pocket folder</u>!

    3. Good listening manners, thank yous, etc.

** ALWAYS TURN IN YOUR TALLY SHEET TO <u>YOUR</u> TEACHER AT THE END OF THE DAY!

_____ Points 1.   **HANDWRITING:** (56 Possible points) Writing a paragraph using all small letters and writing all capital letters correctly.

_____ Points 2.   **MATH:** (219 Possible points) Worksheets on +, --, x, and --. Also several enrichment worksheets.

_____ Points 3.   **SPELLING:** (40 Possible points) Take a 40 word spelling test to see how you compare to other students in all of Rochester, MN.

_____ Points 4.   **LANGUAGE ARTS/SPELLING:** (40 Possible points) Use each of the 40 review words for your spelling units 25-30 in a sentence. One point for each perfect sentence. PROOFREAD!!!!!!!!!!

_____ Points 5.   **SILENT READING:** (90 Possible points) Every 15 minutes of U.S.S.R. (Uninterrupted Sustained Silent Reading) is good for 10 points. That means **ZERO** talking and **REAL** reading!

_____ Points 6.   **LANGUAGE ARTS/RESEARCH:** (60 Possible points) Research an animal of your choice, take notes, write up a report using <u>new</u> facts that you learned. Indent paragraphs, neat writing required.
   **Extra 15 points for a nice illustration.

_____ Points 7.   **CREATIVE WRITING:** (60 Possible points) Write a story, proofread it, and do a final copy. Maybe even a poem????
   **Extra 15 points for a nice illustration.

_____ Points 8.   **ALPHABETIZE A LIST:** (30 Possible points)

POINTS ACCUMULATION PROJECT
(STUDENT TALLY SHEET)

FIRST & LAST NAME:_____

_____ Points 9.   **DICTIONARY LOOK UP:** (20 Possible points) Look up 10 words in the dictionary for 10 points. An **extra 10 points** will be given if you write the definition for the 10 words.

_____ Points 10. **MAP SKILLS:** (50 Possible points) Put the two letter abbreviation for each of the 50 United States on the map in the right place. ****Extra 50 points** for writing the capitals of each state next to its name.

_____ Points 11. **PHY. ED.:** (100 Possible points) <u>Run laps</u>. Each lap is worth one point. <u>Jump rope</u>. Every 30 jumps <u>without a miss</u> is one point.

_____ Points 12. **GAME SHEETS:** (1/2 point for each correct answer) Six different game fun sheets. Do any or all.

_____ Points 13. **LETTER WRITING:** (60 Possible points) Write a letter to someone using the 5 parts of a letter in the correct form as found in your Language Arts Textbook on p. 228. ****Extra 15 points** for a properly addressed envelope as found in your Lang. Arts Textbook on p. 231.

_____ Points 14. **MUSICAL BELLS:** (10 Possible points) Play at least two songs with the bells <u>without mistakes</u>. Do this with a partner and check each other. Help each other learn. LIMIT OF 2 AT A TIME.

_____ Points 15. **MUSIC APPRECIATION VIDEO:** (20 Possible points) View a video, listen to a cassette tape while viewing a flip chart, and take a short quiz on what you have learned. LIMIT OF 20 AT A TIME.

_____ Points 16. **ART:** (20 Possible points) Create an animal collage out of squares, circles, triangles, ovals, and rectangle shapes. LIMIT OF 5 AT A TIME.

_____ Points 17.

	*This space for Auction Day
	_____ TOTAL POINTS TO SPEND
	=_____ SUBTRACT YOUR BID
	_____ TOTAL POINTS LEFT TO SPEND
	=_____ SUBTRACT YOUR BID
	_____ TOTAL POINTS LEFT TO SPEND
	=_____ SUBTRACT YOUR BID
	_____ TOTAL POINTS LEFT TO SPEND
	=_____ SUBTRACT YOUR BID
	_____ TOTAL POINTS LEFT TO SPEND

a._____TOTAL POINTS FROM PAGE 1
+b._____TOTAL POINTS FROM PAGE 2
_____ADD LINES a. and b. TOGETHER
_____SUBTRACT ANY PENALTY POINTS

_____ TOTAL POINTS YOU HAVE TO SPEND AT AUCTION

```
┌─────────────────────────────────────────────┐
│        *This space for Auction Day            │
│                                               │
│  _____ TOTAL POINTS TO SPEND          │
│ -_____ SUBTRACT YOUR BID              │
│  _____ TOTAL POINTS LEFT TO SPEND     │
│ -_____ SUBTRACT YOUR BID              │
│  _____ TOTAL POINTS LEFT TO SPEND     │
│ -_____ SUBTRACT YOUR BID              │
│  _____ TOTAL POINTS LEFT TO SPEND     │
│ -_____ SUBTRACT YOUR BID              │
│  _____ TOTAL POINTS LEFT TO SPEND     │
└─────────────────────────────────────────────┘
```

This project designed and tested
by Dave Bailey, 1989-91

DOLLAR DAYS

1. Art Station

_____   A.   Color Designs. 1 sheet per person $25.00

_____   B.   Name Mobiles $40.00

_____   C.   Nature Art $15.00

_____   D.   Triangle Art $10.00

2. Word Searches $1.00 per 2 words found

_____   A.   State Nicknames $25.00

_____   B.   Nutritionally Correct $15.00

_____   C.   Inclement Weather $12.00

_____   D.   President's Facts $9.00

3. Mazes

_____   A.   Squirrel $5.00

_____   B.   Ski Slope $5.00

4. Cross Patch $1.00 per word

_____   A.   Parrots $14.00

_____   B.   Homework $15.00

5. "Audubon Adventures" $2.00 per answer

_____   A.   April/May 1987 $24.00

_____   B.   June/July 1987 $32.00

6. Creative Writing

_____   A.   Write a 250 word editorial against "vandalism" –
                 use pamphlet for your information. $60.00

_____   B.   The spy (Rough & Final Copy) $75.00

_____   C.   Hockey (Rough & Final Copy) $75.00

7. **Minnesota Map Work**

_____ A. Population Chart $15.00

_____ B. State Parks $20.00

_____ C. Distance Table $52.00

8. **Math**

_____ A. Worksheet 46E $16.00

_____ B. Worksheet 48E $42.00

_____ C. Worksheet 50E $21.00

_____ D. Worksheet 49E $30.00

9. **Free Reading**

_____ A. 30 minutes free reading

10. **Handwriting - Copy the paragraph twice. $10.00**

11. **Newspaper**

_____ A. Page 9, actions 1-2 $10.00

_____ B. Page 39, actions 1-3 $15.00

_____ C. Page 41, actions 1-2 $10.00

12. **Encyclopedia**

_____ A. Scavenger hunt $15.00

13. **Proof Reading**

_____ A. Capitalization and Punctuation $34.00

14. **Word Search II**

_____ A. Use graph paper to design your own word search, words from units 20-25 (basic list) maximum of 30 words. $30.00

15. **Collage**

_____ A. Using pictures from magazines and one central theme, "Me" $15.00

"My parents always told me that people will never know how long it takes you to do something. They will only know how well it is done."

Nancy Hanks

Chapter VII - Volunteers

INTRODUCTION

Volunteers can be a tremendous time saver and source of help if used correctly. Don't be afraid to delegate. One person cannot do it all as well as several. Identify what others can and are willing to do. You will need to plan and develop the use of this resource.

Volunteers can free you for planning and individual, remedial, or extension work with/for students.

Many students, parents, administrators, and other community members are just waiting to be called on to be of assistance.

"Due to classroom management, organizational management, and being positively productive, reinforces you even more to push towards excellence."

Karen Heimer

VOLUNTEERS

Volunteers are like Fords,
   they have better ideas.
Volunteers are like Coke,
   they're the real thing.
Volunteers are like Pan Am,
   they make the going great.
Volunteers are like Pepsi,
   they've got a lot to give.
Volunteers are like Dial Soap,
   they care more.
Don't you wish everyone did?
Volunteers are like VO 5 Hairspray,
   their goodness hold in all weather.
Volunteers are like Hallmark Cards,
   they care enough to give the very best.
Volunteers are like Standard Oil,
   you expect more and you get it.
But most of all,
   Volunteers are like Frosted Flakes,
   They're Grrrrreat!!!!!!!

       Anonymous

**SUGGESTED
LIST**

An example list of ways volunteers might be used:

* Correct weekly spelling tests and record the scores.

* Correct papers that were redone.

* Read to the students.

* Listen to children read.

* Listen to book reports.

* Work one-on-one with skills that need reinforcing such as spelling, math, handwriting, etc.

* Give quizzes.

* Help students with make-up work and tests.

* Take students to the computer lab to supervise (not instruct)

* Put up and take down displays and bulletin boards.

* Run off copies on the duplicator machine after prior training and permission from the office.

* Call to set up field trips, make arrangements, and schedule other parents into occasional work times.

* Do typing for you.

* Make up teaching materials and games, i.e., spelling lists, flash cards, station activities, art materials, etc.

**SIGN-UP
LIST**

Set out a sign-up list for volunteers during the first "Meet the Teacher" day. Meet once with all the volunteers to establish your ground-rule expectations. This meeting should be at the start of the year. Go over the what and how of things clearly. Everyone hears the same thing and has a chance to decline if they wish.

(Volunteers)

YEAR'S SCHEDULE

Make out a year's schedule for what volunteers will be working with, expectations, commitments, etc. and give to each volunteer. Communications are clear and misunderstandings are averted.

VOLUNTEER'S BASKET

Put out a basket just for volunteers. Put their name on it and number the requests by priority. Establish a schedule each week that can be counted on. Dependability is a necessity that must be cultivated. Don't forget thank yous and small gifts of appreciation.

WORK AT HOME

Send things home for the volunteers to do in their home. They can manage their schedules easier, save travel time, and they don't have to dress up as much. Keep communication open so that they don't feel neglected, overworked, under informed, etc.

GUIDE SHEET

Use a simple guide sheet for volunteers. Set up a place where they can find these directions without you having to take time to explain what you want done. The three easy sections might include: Tasks with students, Tasks on their own, and a section for written comments and feedback. **(See example "A", p. 122)**

WRITTEN DIRECTIONS

Save communication time by writing out the directions for volunteers. They then check off the work on the list when completed. **(See examples "B" and "C", pp. 123, 124)**

AREAS OUT OF REACH

Have volunteers display art work in areas inaccessible to students: on board strips too high for students, locked display cases, and various areas in the hallway.

HELPFUL INFORMATION

Have a volunteer collect information and coordinate into a useful tool. An example might be 3 x 5 cards with student names, addresses, telephone numbers, birthdates, siblings, etc. It is a practical reference to save you time looking up information each time you need it.

A.V. FOR THE YEAR

Check off all the Audio Visual materials you will be using for the school year, such as tapes, films, filmstrips, etc. Have a volunteer fill out the forms with the titles and numbers. You just fill in the dates and mail them to the A.V. Center.

ORGANIZING MATERIALS

Volunteers can be used well to file worksheets and materials well ahead of time for the entire year. They are a great help in organizing and sorting.

REPRODUCTION OF MATERIALS	Keep a folder for what needs to be reproduced. The volunteer runs off these copies once a week for the following week. It saves you a lot of time standing around by the machine.
PARENT SPEAKERS	Use **parent speakers** for related subject areas. It adds variety, interest, and is great for personal relations. Think of the pride in the parent's child.
PAPERS	Take-home papers can be sorted and stapled into booklets by a volunteer. This makes a well-received parent packet once a week. Grandparents love it, too.
TECHNOLOGY HELP	The volunteer is a great help when it comes to technology. They can help the students tape record, work on the computer, and run various audio-visual equipment.
DEVELOPING MATERIALS	Put volunteers in charge of making flashcards, math games, reading games, and other time-consuming projects. The final touch includes having them laminate the materials for durability and reusability.
"THANK YOU"	Don't forget to thank your volunteers with appropriate praise, encouragement, remembrances, and notes. **(See example "D", p. 125)**
EXTRA HELP	Take all the extra help you can get. Delegation is wonderful. Don't expect it to be "exactly" like you would have done it, but empowerment and trust will get more done in the long run. It takes time to train, encourage, and thank others. However, you will gain all kinds of time in the long run. Gain production through aides, volunteers, special area teachers, student teachers, parents, older students in the school, administration, etc.
OLDER STUDENTS	Use older students from the high schools as volunteers. See if there is a **"CAP's" Program** in your district (Community Awareness Program). Students who are exploring career choices would benefit by this experience.

NOTES:

"Most kids hear waht you say;

some kids do what you say;

but all kids do what you do."

- Kathleen Casey Theisen -

DAY

Kid Tasks

1.

2.

3.

4.

Other

1.

2.

3.

4.

Your comments:

MONDAY VOLUNTEERS

Kahty:

____   Check Terri, Ben, Destiny, Molly on addition facts and addition families.

____   Recheck spelling, pre-test, check on green record sheet.

____   Cut green construction paper 6 x 9, 60 sheets and staple seed booklets.

Travis:

____   Proximity monitor.

____   Assist Mrs. Ostby.

____   Hang all falling stuff off of walls.

____   Hang string and hooks from ceiling in cluster in art corner, (28).

____   Sort papers in this basket.

Terry:

____   Fix math notebook into order (throw extras).

____   Type math helpers letter.

____   Type Young Astronaut lists.

____   Staple and record D.O.L. papers.

Darlene:

____   Tutor Destiny and Ben in math.

____   Tutor Molly and Terri in math.

TO DO LIST

Example "C"

COMPLETED

DATE _____

1. ☐
2. ☐
3. ☐
4. ☐
5. ☐
6. ☐
7. ☐
8. ☐
9. ☐
10. ☐
11. ☐
12. ☐
13. ☐
14. ☐

TO DO LIST

COMPLETED

DATE _____

1. ☐
2. ☐
3. ☐
4. ☐
5. ☐
6. ☐
7. ☐
8. ☐
9. ☐
10. ☐
11. ☐
12. ☐
13. ☐
14. ☐

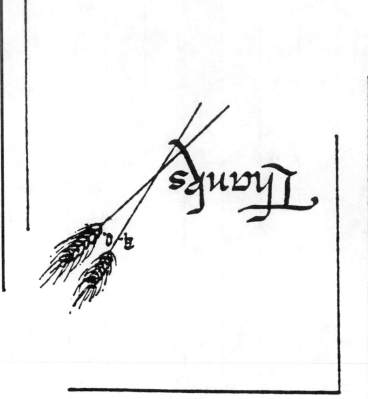

Thanks

--Fold here--

--Fold here--

Your child
is
one of the

reasons

I enjoy

teaching !

Chapter VIII - Personal Relations and Newsletters

TEACHER PLEASE NOTE: Please be aware that many of the ideas shared by teachers can and do transcend across several grade levels. Be sure to read all grades' suggestions in order to profit from the many other excellent ideas.

INTRODUCTION

Any effort above the minimum requirements of the classroom will be noticed and appreciated by many -- both in and out of the classroom.

Good personal relationships will save time by having fewer discipline problems, you'll have more parent and administrator support, and you'll feel better about yourself.

Sell yourself. You're in a "people business." It's not so much what you, but how you do it. Establish open and honest communications. You will prevent misinformation and at the same time set up the ground work for effectively dealing with problems.

This chapter shows what other teachers do to promote personal relations and keep parents informed through newsletters.

"It's nice to be important, but it's more important to be nice."

John Cassis

NOTES:

"This time, like all times, is a very good one, if we but know what to do with it."

Ralph Waldo Emerson

DRAW A PICTURE	Have each child in the room draw a picture of the **"Special Child of the Week."** On the same sheet of paper, have them list all the special things about that child, i.e., color of hair, eyes, likes, etc. Talk about all the things that make the child so special. The children sign their pictures on the back and put them in a folder for the child to take home on Friday. The folder can be a double-sized colored construction paper folded in half. You can print the child's name repetitively around the outside edges and print **"YOU ARE SPECIAL"** in the middle. If you can coordinate with birthdays, classmates can make birthday cards.
PHONE CALLS	Phone calling two children each night builds a very solid relationship with the child and gains support from the parents. It helps first graders to talk. It only takes 5 minutes per call.
NEWSLETTERS	Give students a blank sheet of paper headed **"NEWSLETTER."** They write: **"PLEASE ASK ME ABOUT:_____"** and two or three new learning activities each week, which allows parents to see what is being studied, reinforce their child's learning, view their child's handwriting progress, and note any weak areas. Student ideas and ownership is important; also a discussion of answers at school reinforces the success at home as well as better retention.
DAY'S SCHEDULE	Send home a copy of your normal teaching day's schedule and invite parents to visit your room. **(See example "A", p. 141)**
SMALL GROUP CONFERENCES	Have a small group conference with five families at a time. Provide each parent with a folder showing the child's work. Include material to show personal information, social development, physical development, academic skills of strength and need, and any areas of concern.
QUESTIONS	Give parents a list of most commonly asked questions. Have them ready before conferences and send them home to act as a springboard for conference discussion. The parent can take the initiative to target the ones they don't know or are most concerned about. You will be more at ease having anticipated most inquiries. **(See example "B", p. 142)**

NOTES:

"Unless you're getting more out of your job than what you're putting in, maybe you're in the wrong job."

Don Valentine (1989)
A Rochester Principal

STUDENT INFORMATION

At the beginning of the year have students write an autobiography about themselves. They can also illustrate it with a self-characterization. Don't forget to do one, yourself. Perhaps you want to speed up finding out about them by having them simply fill in an **"All About Me"** booklet with specific questions and blanks to answer.

YEAR'S SCRAPBOOK

Keep diaries to be written in periodically. These are kept, along with awards, special papers, flat art projects, etc. that the children collect all year. They are made into a scrapbook as a remembrance of the entire year. The project is announced at the beginning of the year, reinforced, and makes an excellent project in the spring.

NOTES

Have students write thank you notes and invitations in their own handwriting instead of a typed, office copy. Parents will appreciate the emphasis on neatness and the **"personal touch."**

UNIT INFORMATION

Written communique can be strengthened with introductory letters to units listing the learner outcomes, mastery updates on each student in between conferences or grading, end-of-chapter or level notes, and personal notes to emphasize positives or a concern. A **"Homework Alert"** for late assignments may require a parent's signature the next morning. **(See examples "C" and "D", pp. 143, 144))**

"TICKET TO GO HOME"

Remember the student who replies "Nothing," to the parent's question: "What did you learn in school today?" You can solve that easily with a **"Ticket to Go Home."** Have a short half sheet form with a name blank and **"This is what I learned today"** followed by blank lines. Pupils fill this out in the last 5 minutes of the day along with written feedback to you, on the back side, being optional. They have to be specific; "Math" is not acceptable. A math problem with the answer, is. Collect them as they go out the door. Look them over and have the student take them home the next night. Parents love it and you get a good picture of what's going through their minds.

"PASS"

Send home a **"Pass"** or a **"Ticket to Disembark."** Each student writes one or two new things that he/she learned that day on a special **"Pass."** It must be turned in before they leave that afternoon. Parents won't have to get the "Nothin" answer to their question: "What did you learn in school today?" **(See example "E", p. 145)**

"HELP LETTER"

Send home a **"help letter"** to give students one-on-one extra practice time. **(See example "F", p. 146)** Add extra meaning by having the principal's support and signature.

"CONVERSA-TIONAL NEWSLETTERS"

Try **"Conversational Newsletters."** These are a list of questions for the parents to discuss with their child regarding a certain story they have just read in reading class. Send them home with the students and solicit parent comments to see if they are being used. Parents will have another opportunity to get involved in a positive way.

"RADIO THEATER"

Set up and do a **"Radio Theater"** with your students. Have stools in front for all the actors and ready a short script for each small group of students. Videotape it for use outside the room for parents to watch while they are waiting for their conference. Students will enjoy checking it out during the year to take home to share with their families and grandparents. Incorporate the videotape into speeches, reports, science projects, art work, music, demonstrations, etc.

"Every student caring, means every student sharing."

Dave Bailey

CHILDREN'S WRITING

Make each child responsible for writing an article for a newspaper for parents. The edition is sent home after volunteer parents type it up and print copies for each family. Perhaps have each child take turns writing a paragraph for your weekly newsletters.

CAMPOUT

Planning and taking the students on an outdoor educational campout overnight gets parents involved and provides an experience many children never have a chance to have.

CHAPERON

The very best P.R. is an "Outdoor Educational Campout." Parents are involved as chaperons, and the event is forever memorable. Use the curriculum to make or present something to the parents. Plan an art project, program, gift, card, etc. Seasonal themes are perfect.

STUDENTS' NEWSLETTERS

Assign students to develop and publish your newsletters. Assign different topic areas along with current events happening at school. Putting it on a word processor allows for easy proofing and printing. Students take ownership for their product, learning is heightened, and parents love it.

UNIT INFORMATION --- PERSONALIZE IT

Keep parents informed about the units you are covering so that they feel part of the learning process and can reinforce your teaching. Some may even find ways to help supply things for the classroom. By writing your notes of information in long hand, you make it more personal and save time going to the typewriter or computer. Just sign it once and run copies. **(See example "G", p. 147)**

NOTES:

"The needs for safety, belongingness, love relations, and for respect can be satisfied only by <u>other people</u>, i.e.; only from outside the person. This means considerable dependence on the environment."

Abraham Maslow (1968)
<u>*Toward a Psychology of Being*</u>

**GOALS/
OBJECTIVES**

Develop a pamphlet with your personal goals and objectives. Use this as an introductory hand out for visitors and at open house in the fall. The Apple program called "Print Shop" makes an ideal greeting card with graphics and borders right on the computer. You just type in your information on the keyboard and run copies off. **(See example "H", p. 148)**

**POSITIVE
COMMENTS**

On "Meet the Teacher" night, pass out 3 x 5 cards and have the parents write positive things on them that their child does. It will give you lots of positive information to build from in the following year.

VOLUNTEERS

On the night of that first fall open house, put out a slip for parents to sign in on. Have a space for telephone numbers and if they would like to volunteer to help throughout the year and for what types of things. You will know who came and also save yourself lots of telephone calls trying to get helpers later on. The list will be "ready-made."

PICTURES

Take pictures of major activities throughout the year. Put them on a large poster board with a short informational caption under each. Display them in the hall for the public, parents, and children to enjoy and remember.

**"SPECIAL
CHILD OF
THE WEEK"**

Create a **"Special Child of the Week"** bulletin board. They can bring in pictures and prized possessions to share with their classmates. Have them bring in a pillow case for the class to sign. A parent volunteer can go over all the names with tube paint to set and make the names permanent. This is a nice memento.

**STUDENT'S
SCRAPBOOK**

Students have a year-long file for certificates, creative writings, star papers, art work, etc. These are then bound as a scrapbook and taken home the last week of school to keep in a safe place for enjoyment in years to come.

**VIDEOTAPE
THE YEAR**

Videotape the students throughout the year. Special projects, first day of school, programs, field trips, etc. At the end of the year, parents can send a blank tape in and the video is reproduced as a video-scrap book.

VIDEOTAPE MAJOR PROJECTS	Videotape students doing a major project of some sort. At the end of the year parents can copy it on a blank tape as a momento. Parents may check out the tape for 2-3 days during the last month of school or you could take an order and sell them "at cost." Show it to "waiting parents" on conference days or during open house, also.
PARENT HELP	Have a file of **"parent activities"** they may do with their child at home. When asked, you can target certain areas of the curriculum on-the-spot. Parents will feel more involved and part of "the team." You will come off looking well-organized and competent.
PARENT/ CHILD LUNCH	Invite parents to come to the school to visit shortly before lunch time and to take their child out for lunch once a year. That student is the focus of attention for that day or week.
"OPEN DOOR" POLICY	Have an open door policy. Teach with your door open. Invite parents to stop by anytime as a show of confidence and warmth. Send your teaching schedule home so parents know what you're doing. If a parent comes to bring the student something or pick them up, ask if they have a few minutes to sit and observe.
PARENT VISITS	Parents become very supportive when they know what you are doing. Encourage each parent to get into your room to observe at least once during the year to see you in the process of instruction.
SEND INFORMA- TION HOME	Send learner outcomes and students' results home. Pre and post test scores show progress and a structured, planned curriculum. Parents like to regularly know what is going on with their child, and many parents reinforce the curriculum and positive assessments at home.
QUARTERLY REPORT	Send home a quarterly report for parents. Keep records on the computer and it will be easy to just add to it each time. **(See example "I", p. 149)**
PROBLEMS	Always deal with problems with <u>all</u> parties present. This prevents miscommunications and gives everyone a chance to defend themselves and hear the same thing.

TEAM CONFERENCES   Teachers who team together should do parent conferencing together. Joint conferences with 2-3 teachers, the parents, and the child adds productively to the conference. Teachers see the child in different ways. It takes more time, but the quality yields stronger parent support. Emphasis is on informing, truth, positive attitude, strengths, gifted areas, and planning for next-step growth areas.

HOME CONFERENCES   Every other year, make home-bound conferences an option for the parents. These are in lieu of the school-based, scheduled ones. Once you have been on "their turf," it is easier to understand the child and see them in their normal setting. You gain a lot of respect from the parents for going the extra mile.

OUT-OF-SCHOOL ACTIVITIES   When your students are involved, attend outside-of-school student activities such as youth sports, plays, church presentations, etc. You'll have fewer discipline problems when families and students know you care.

INVITE SCHOOL BOARD MEMBERS   Invite school board members into your room. This shows a confident nature. School board members appreciate being involved by invitation.

"JOINT AGREEMENT"   Don't confuse children. Talk with each individual parent and ask how they "deal" with their child for behavior, etc. Then explain your beliefs and establish a **"joint agreement."** A consensus through understanding creates a solid front in one direction.

PHONE CALLS   Having a phone in the classroom not only saves lots of steps, but encourages quick phone calls for any problem or concern before it gets larger or forgotten. Just have the secretary screen the incoming calls or take messages during teaching time.

STUDENT PHONE CALLS   For immediate reinforcement of something positive that takes no teacher time, have the student go to the telephone and call the parent and inform them of something that happened special. Keep a class list near the phone to check off so that the calls are an equal number per student throughout the year.

PHONE CONTACT	Try to make a phone contact with every family once a quarter if you don't see them under normal day-to-day conditions sometime throughout the quarter. Perhaps run some make-up work over to their house on the way home. The personal touch can go a long way toward good feelings and less discipline problems.
PHONE ONCE/ SEMESTER	Call each parent once per semester if you don't have other contacts with them outside of conferences. Review goals and ask if there are any questions or concerns. It keeps the lines of communication open and wards off trouble before it escalates.
MISSED CONFERENCES	Call any parents who miss conferences and review their child's grades. Answering any questions or concerns may save you a problem later. It shows concern and caring on your part.
OPEN CALLS	Be open enough to encourage phone calls at home. If a student has questions about homework he/she should have your number and blessing to call.
"PARENT'S CALL NIGHT"	Set up a **"Parent's Call Night"** when they are encouraged to call <u>you</u> about any comments, questions, or concerns. Inform through a newsletter. Extending yourself outside the workplace is professional. Parents won't harbor concerns if they talk about them right away, and won't have any excuse if they don't.
POSITIVE REINFORCEMENT	Putting students into groups allows you to reinforce positive things that they do by putting their group number on the board. Students start to encourage each other to do the "right" things. Any productive behavior such as noise level, cooperative group work, clean area, etc. can be highlighted and rewarded.
WEEKLY HAPPY-O-GRAM	Ensure that each child gets a weekly Happy-O-Gram by writing each child's name at the top of a blank at the beginning of each week. That way you won't forget anyone. **(See example "J", p. 150)**

**PERSONAL
NOTES**

Try to write five personal notes to students or parents each day. Make them positive in terms of reminders or things that are special. Keep a checklist so that every child receives an equal number of notes in a set period of time. Include comments about what the child is doing outside of school, also. This gives feedback and shows your level of interest in, and knowledge of, individuals.

**CLASS
PROGRAM**

Develop a school program to be presented by your class to parents and relatives. Invitations are written by the children. Perhaps a refreshment time in the cafeteria to meet everyone afterwards could be included. This once-a-year emphasis will be talked about in years to come.

**CLASS
DINNER**

At Thanksgiving, have a class dinner. Involve as many parents as possible. Art work, background research, and costumes are natural predecessors.

**PARENT/
STUDENT
GIFT**

Make a monthly, seasonal gift for the parent. It could be a paper flower, a card, a picture, or various art projects. Christmas and Mother's Day are naturals.

**"WORD FOR
THE DAY"**

Have a **"Word for the Day."** Parents know this expectation and are encouraged to get involved by asking about it each evening. Anytime parents feel part of the team, everyone wins.

**ROOM NAME
PLATES**

Have teacher name plates extend perpendicularly out from the wall next to their room. This allows their name plate to be seen from some distance and doesn't depend upon the door being open or shut to see the teacher's name. This makes it very easy for a parent visiting to locate their child's teacher.

**COMPUTER
FORM**

Newsletters (preferably weekly) have been lauded and encouraged by most parents. Just an indication of what's going on at school in different subjects is helpful. Get as creative as you wish. A blank form designed on a computer can just be filled in and run off quick. Run it on the same color paper each week so it can be spotted fast. This saves calls to you by the overly-concerned parent and gives you a forum to stress areas to reinforce at home. Giving students positive strokes will get the students reading them, too. Try publishing student writings on the back side.
(See example "K", p. 151)

138

YOUR OWN LOGO Design your own logo for newsletters, or make 50 copies of the school's letterhead before school starts. If you sign them before you run them off you've just saved yourself 50 signatures. The Apple program called "Print Shop" makes a one-sheet "poster" which graphically lends itself perfectly to a one-sheet newsletter format. Run enough blanks for the year -- and beyond. **(See example "L", p. 152)**

MONTHLY NEWSLETTER CALENDAR Send home a monthly newsletter calendar. All special events are noted on a blank calendar and sent home as a reminder and notice. Quotations are a nice filler and also get a message across. Use the back for additional parent information, etc.
(See examples "M", "N", and "O", pp. 153-155)

ANSWER QUESTIONS Keep and add to a list of **"Most commonly asked questions."** Go over the answers to these in newsletters and at the first conference of the school year. Anticipation always saves time later on. **(See example "B", p. 142)**

STUDENT DRAWINGS Include one or two student **drawings** (reduced on a copying Machine if necessary) to embellish your newsletters and things sent home to parents.

PERSONAL COMMENTS Put personal comments in your newsletters, using students' names. Underline them. It sets a tone of importance and will broaden the number who read it.

STUDENTS' CREATIVE WRITINGS Include one or two students' **creative writings** in your newsletters. Reduce them in size on the Savin Machine and put them on the back side. Students will start reading them more and will encourage parents to do the same.

STUDENT PROFILE Include a profile about a different student with each newsletter. Tell their interests, likes, personality, etc. It makes that child and family feel proud and special. Try to coincide with the pupil's birthday week if possible.

WRITTEN NEWSLETTERS Write parent communications just one time as you are thinking about it. The longhand messages make them more personal and you don't have to make a trip to the computer or typewriter. Just sign them and run off as many copies as you wish.

JOURNAL NEWSLETTER Take a little time at the end of each day to write down major things accomplished that day. It is like a journal. At the end of the week, run copies off and send them home.
(See example "P", p. 156)

STUDENT PROJECT Write newsletters for parents as a class. Students can illustrate them, show off their handwriting, and effectively review what has been happening in the classroom. A great language arts activity.

STUDENT INVOLVEMENT Research says that if the students have input into the layout of the newsletter, it will more likely be read. Use the same heading each time. Several teachers on your team may take turns each week to spread out the responsibility.
(See example "Q", p. 157)

FILE A COPY Give a copy of any teacher newsletters and parent communication to the principal and don't forget to keep a file copy for yourself. Have someone proofread them before copying.

SPACE FOR PARENT REQUEST At the bottom of your weekly newsletters, provide a place where parents can write back with requests, comments, questions, and sign that they received the newsletter.

"If you treat an individual as he is, he will remain as he is. But if you treat him as if he were what he ought to be and could be, he will become what he ought to be and could be."

Goethe

CLASSROOM SCHEDULE

1st Grade   19___ - 19___
_____   School _____

Time					
8:45 8:55	Opening Attendance	Opening Lunch Count	Opening Announcements	Opening - Song ----	Opening Planning
8:55 9:45	Reading	Reading	Reading	Reading	Reading
9:45 10:30	Reading	Reading	Reading	Reading	Reading
10:30 10:55	Reading Language Arts	Reading Language Arts	Reading Language Arts	Reading Language Arts	Reading Language Arts
10:55	Phy.Ed. ✻	Phy.Ed. (Classroom Teacher)	Phy.Ed. —————	Phy.Ed. ————→	Phy.Ed. ✻
11:20 11:25	Get Ready for lunch	——————————————————————————————————————→			
11:25 12:20	Lunch	Lunch (Noon duty) 12:00-12:20	Lunch	Lunch	Lunch
12:20 12:30	Attendance Planning	————————————————————————————————————→			
12:30 1:00	Math	Music ✻	Math	Music ✻	Math
1:00 1:30	PIC	PIC	PIC	PIC	PIC
1:30 2:00	PIC	MATH	✻(1:20 - 2:10) Art - Every Other week	MATH	PIC
2:00 2:30	DAP	DAP	PIC	DAP	Library ✻
2:30 3:05	Literature Sharing-MON	Language Arts		Language Arts	Literature Sharing-FRI
3:05 3:10	Evaluation	————————————————————————————————————→			
3:15	Dismiss	————————————————————————————————————→			

141